Folens History Book

Industry, Reform and Empire

Britain 1750–1900

Aaron Wilkes

go to pg 21

Author's acknowledgements

The author wishes to acknowledge Peter Burton and Nina Randall of Folens Publishers for their advice during the preparation of this book. He also wishes to thank his teaching colleague James Clayton for his practical suggestions and task preparation. He is particularly indebted to his wife, Emma, for the support she has given.

© 2004 Folens Limited, on behalf of the author.

United Kingdom: Folens Publishers, Apex Business Centre, Boscombe Road, Dunstable, LU5 4RL.
Email: folens@folens.com

Ireland: Folens Publishers, Greenhills Road, Tallaght, Dublin 24.
Email: info@folens.ie

Poland: JUKA, ul. Renesansowa 38, Warsaw 01-905.

Editor: Nina Randall

Series design, page layout and illustrations: Neil Sutton, Pumpkin House Cambridge

Picture researcher: Sue Sharp

Cover design: 2idesign Ltd., Cambridge

First published 2004 by Folens Limited.

Every effort has been made to trace the copyright holders of material used in this publication. If any copyright holder has been overlooked, we should be pleased to make any necessary arrangements.

British Library Cataloguing in Publication Data. A catalogue record for this publication is available from the British Library.

ISBN 1 84303 409 3

Acknowledgements

Art Directors & Trip Photo Library: 41 (right and bottom left), 112; Boston Irish Tourism Association: 73; Bridgeman Art Library: 5, 76 (right), 83; Bridgeman Art Library/Alexander Turnbull Library, Wellington, New Zealand: 66; Bridgeman Art Library/British Library: 80; Bridgeman Art Library/Courtesy of the Trustees of Sir John Soane's Museum, London: 89; Bridgeman Art Library/ Guildhall Library, Corporation of London, UK: 44; Bridgeman Art Library/Harris Museum and Art Gallery, Preston, Lancashire, UK: 92; Bridgeman Art Library/Ironbridge Gorge Museum, Telford, Shropshire, UK: 24; Bridgeman Art Library/ Marylebone Cricket Club, London, UK: 114; Bridgeman Art Library/Royal College of Surgeons, London, UK: 101; Bridgeman Art Library/Royal Geographical Society, London, UK: 69; Bridgeman Art Library/Royal Holloway and Bedford New College, Surrey, UK: 37, 111; Bridgeman Art Library/Stapleton Collection: 45; Bridgeman Art Library/ Wilberforce House, Hull City Museums and Art Galleries, UK: 75, 79 (both); British Library: 68; Corbis Images: 123; Hulton Archive: 13, 15, 98, 105, 110; Mary Evans Picture Library: 22, 34, 35 (left), 41 (top Left), 53, 54, 59, 60, 62, 76 (left), 78, 85, 88, 94, 99, 106, 109, 113, 117 (top right), 119, 120; Mirror Syndication International: 63; NSPCC: 108; Peter Newark's Pictures: 71; Popperfoto: 121; Punch Cartoon Library: 58; Royal Academy of Arts Picture Library: 93; Royal Archives, Her Majesty Queen Elizabeth II: 86; Science & Society Picture Library: 35 (right), 39, 43, 117 (top left); Sheffield Galleries & Museums Trust: 12 (left); Sheffield Local Studies Library www.picturesheffield.com: 12 (right); Sotherby's Picture Library: 116/117; Statens Museum for Kunst, Copenhagen: 29; Timelife Pictures/Mansell/Getty Images: 21, 115; Wellcome Trust Medical Photograph Library: 96, 102, 103; Western Reserve Historical Society Library, Cleveland, Ohio: 81.

'Britain 1750-1900', Susan Willoughby, Heinemann, 1995: 39; 'British Social and Economic History: Coursework and Questions', Simon Mason, Simon & Schuster Education, 1990: 11; 'History Alive 3, 1789–1914', Peter Moss, Hart-Davis Education Ltd., 1984: 20, 28, 42; 'In Search of History, 1714–1900', J F Aylett, Hodder and Stoughton, 1995: 31, 39; 'Investigating History, Britain 1750–1900', John D Clare, Hodder and Stoughton, 2003: 25, 39, 72 (X2), 91; 'Life in Victorian Britain', Michael St John Parker, Pitkin Guides, 1999: 40; 'Lister as I knew him', J Leeson in 'Health and Medicine, 1750–1900', John Robottom, Longman, 1991: 102; 'Pax Britannica', James Morris, 1968 in 'Expansion, Trade and Industry', Ros Adams, Causeway Press Ltd., 1992: 67; 'Quest: Black Peoples of the Americas', Bea Stimpson, Nelson Thornes, 2001: 77; 'The Changing Face of Britain', Paul Shuter and John Child, Heinemann, 1989: 39; 'The Little Book of British History', Duncan Gunn, Mustard, 1999: 72; 'The Suffragettes and After', J F Aylett, Hodder and Stoughton, 1987: 92; 'The World of Empire, Industry and Trade', Bea Stimpson, Nelson Thornes, 2000: 42 (X2), 70, 72; 'Victorian Britain', Andrew Langley, Hamlyn, 1994: 40, 71; 'Who? What? When? Victorians', Bob Fowke, Hodder Children's books, 2003: 41; 'Work out Social and Economic History', Simon Mason, Blackwell, 1988: 40.

Contents

What was Britain like in 1750?

AIMS

▸ How was Britain governed in 1750?

▸ In what ways was Britain developing into 'Great Britain'?

This book is about the people and events of Britain between 1750 and 1900, a time of great change. For you to see how important these changes were, you must first find out about Britain in 1750. Then, towards the end of this book, you will be asked to compare the Britain of 1750 with the Britain of 1900.

How many people were there?

About seven million people lived in Britain in 1750. However, it's hard to know the exact number because no one ever counted! Instead, historians have estimated the amount by analysing sources like church records. These list the number of baptisms and burials in any one church.

PAUSE FOR THOUGHT

Church records were not always accurate. Can you think of any reasons why they might not be? Clue: A costly registration. What problems does this cause historians?

Who ruled?

In 1750, Britain was made up of England, Scotland and Wales. After Queen Anne (the last of the Stuarts) died in 1714, her German relatives came over to rule the country. However, new King George I didn't speak English and mostly left Parliament alone to rule the country ... which they loved! When George I died, his son (another George) took over.

So in 1750, George II was King (yet he wasn't particularly popular – they said he preferred Germany to England!). Parliament continued to make the laws and held elections every few years. However, in 1750, only 5% of men (the very rich 5%) could vote ... and women couldn't vote at all.

Sir Robert Walpole had No. 10 Downing Street built in 1736. He was one of a group of MPs who worked closely with George II (the King had to agree with all Parliament's decisions before they became law ... but MPs controlled a lot of his money!). MPs teased Walpole for being so close to George II and called him **Prime Minister** as an insult ('prime' means 'first' or 'No. 1'). The nickname stuck and Walpole remained Prime Minister for 21 years. Ten Downing Street is still home to Britain's PM.

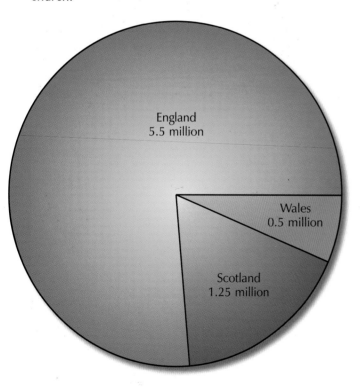

England
5.5 million

Wales
0.5 million

Scotland
1.25 million

▲ **Source A** A pie chart showing the estimated **population** in 1750. England's population was five and a half million; Wales' half a million and Scotland's one and a quarter million. Ireland's population was about three million.

FACT: ▶ Cruel and crazy Germans

▶ From 1714 to 1820, three men named George were the kings of Great Britain and Ireland:

▶ George I (1714–1727): Loved Germany and spent most of his time there. Famous for treating his wife very badly. He had lots of lovers but hated it when his wife Dorothea had one herself. The King ordered Dorothea's lover to leave England – which he did ... or so she thought! Years later, workmen found her lover's dead body under floorboards in Dorothea's bedroom!

▶ George II (1727–1760): Son of George I. Also loved Germany and spent lots of his time there. He was the last British king to lead his army into battle against the French ... again!

▼ A painting of George III, King from 1760 to 1820. He was the best known German ruler and was King for the majority of the period covered in this book.

▶ George III (1760–1820): Grandson of George II. Spoke English with no German accent and never visited Germany. First king to live in Buckingham Palace. Loved the simple life and enjoyed working on his farms. People called him 'Farmer George'. Sadly, he suffered from periods of madness, during which time he ended every sentence with the word 'peacock'. He once carried a pillowcase around with him for weeks and occasionally declared himself dead!

FACT: ▶ United Kingdom?

▶ Ireland was a conquered land so all major laws were made by the British Parliament in London. Ireland joined to form the United Kingdom in 1801 under the Act of Union.

How did people die?

People didn't know that germs caused disease. Basic operations, like removing an infected toenail, could result in death because there were no painkillers or germ-free, clean, operating rooms.

The big killer diseases were smallpox (highly infectious, causing fever, blisters, scabs ... and then death!) and respiratory diseases, which affected breathing and the lungs, for example, pneumonia, bronchitis, diphtheria and tuberculosis.

The average age of death in Britain in 1750 was about 30 years of age. For every 1 000 babies born, over 150 would die before they reached their first birthday ... and one in five of the mothers would die too!

▼ Milkmaids sold milk around the city streets in open-top buckets. One customer wrote in his diary that on its journey around the city, the milk collected 'spit, snot, dirt, rubbish, sick and lice'. Enjoy your drink!

How did people get around?

Slowly – very slowly. There were no aeroplanes, trains or cars. Most people rarely left their village except to go to the local town on market day. The roads were so bad that it could take up to two weeks to travel from London to Edinburgh ... and four days to get from London to Exeter (and it's only 140 miles away!). Some roads had been improved, but in 1750, they were a rare sight.

▼ **Source B** Adapted from the journals of Queen Anne in 1704. They were travelling from Windsor (in Berkshire) to Petworth (in Sussex), a distance of about 40 miles.

'We set out at six in the morning and didn't get out of the carriages (except when we overturned or got stuck in the mud) for 14 hours. We had nothing to eat and passed through some of the worst roads I ever saw in my life.'

How did people make money?

Eight out of ten people lived and worked in the countryside. They grew food and reared cattle and sheep. They grew enough to feed themselves and perhaps some extra to sell in the local town. Goods were made in people's homes or in small workshops attached to their homes. Some of the larger workshops in towns produced high-quality goods that were sold abroad. But even these businesses employed no more than 50 people. Everything a village or town needed was made by hand or on very simple machines – buttons, needles, woollen or cotton cloth, glass, bricks, pottery, candles and bread.

Some towns were growing fast (Liverpool, Leeds, Birmingham and Glasgow more than doubled in size between 1750 and 1800). Shopkeepers, chimney sweeps, flower-sellers, doctors, housemaids, builders, cobblers and street traders all made a living in these fast growing towns.

 FACT: ▶ Finer china

▶ Some of the world's best-quality fine china was produced by Josiah Wedgwood, based in Stoke on Trent. His goods were sold all over the world.

(!) WISE UP WORDS

population   Prime Minister   imported
exported

How 'Great' was Britain?

By 1750, Britain was becoming a major world power.

- The British controlled areas of land in many other countries. Parts of Canada, the West Indies, Africa, India and America were under British control.

- Britain **imported** Indian silk, jewels, pottery, ivory, tea, American coffee, sugar, tobacco and Canadian cod. Companies sold these around Britain or they were **exported** to other customers abroad.

- The goods made in Britain, like cloth, pottery and iron, were sold abroad in huge numbers. All this trade made a lot of money for British companies and provided plenty of jobs for British workers.

 **HUNGRY FOR MORE?** *Find out how Britain is ruled today. How are important decisions made about your lives on a local, national and world level? What powers does Parliament have? How powerful is today's Prime Minister?*

WORK

1 a Write a sentence or two about the origin of the term 'Prime Minister'.

   b In 1750, who was more powerful – the King or Parliament?

   c Write a sentence or two about your Prime Minister today. Before writing your answer, you may wish to discuss the role of your Prime Minister and their powers.

2 It is 1750. Pretend you are a foreign visitor, sent on a trip to Britain by a foreign king. You must prepare a factfile on Britain for your king back home. Use the following headings to help you:

- The people – How many? Where do they live? What do they do?
- The people in charge – Who runs the country? How? What about the Royal Family?
- Health of the nation – What were the common illnesses and diseases? How long could an average man expect to live?
- Travel – How advanced was Britain's transport system?
- 'Great' Britain – Were the British conquering other lands? If so, where and why?

Present your report as a TOP SECRET document – you never know what a foreign king might need the information for!

1 • Living and working

Why did the population 'explode'?

AIMS

▶ How did Britain's population grow?
▶ What were some of the causes of this increase?

Between 1750 and 1900, the population of Britain grew so fast that one historian called it 'an explosion of people'. There were about seven million people living in Britain in 1750, with another three million in Ireland. By 1900, Britain's population was nearly 40 million. In other words, the population had more than quadrupled! So what was behind this 'explosion'?

▼ **Source A** This graph estimates the population of Britain between 1750 and 1900. Following 1801 and every ten years after, a **census** was taken in England, Wales and Scotland. However, it didn't include Ireland's population.

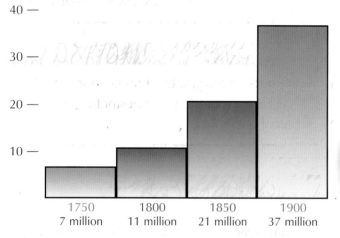

1750	1800	1850	1900
7 million	11 million	21 million	37 million

There are only three possible ways for a population to increase:

i) the number of births can increase

ii) the number of deaths can decrease

iii) **immigrants** can move to the country

Historians know that after 1750, the number of people moving to Britain was similar to the number of people leaving – so **immigration** couldn't have caused the population explosion. This leaves two other explanations.

Your task is to look through the following facts. Each has been identified by a historian as a cause of the population explosion between 1750 and 1900. Try to think whether the information in each fact would:

i) increase the number of births

ii) decrease the number of deaths

iii) do both

Fab farmers

After 1750, farmers produced more food. People had the opportunity to enjoy a healthier diet – fresh vegetables, fruit, meat, potatoes and dairy products. All the protein and vitamins helped the body to fight disease.

Young love

After 1750, people started to get married younger. This gave couples more time to have more children.

Smelly pants

From 1800, cotton started to replace wool as Britain's most popular cloth. Cotton underwear became very popular. Cotton is much easier to wash than wool, so regular washing killed off germs.

Magic midwives

After 1750, there were improvements in the care of pregnant women by **midwives**. Some hospitals were even providing **maternity** beds by 1760.

8

Jenner's jabs

In 1796, Edward Jenner discovered how to vaccinate against one of Britain's worst diseases – smallpox. Gradually, more and more people were treated, until 1870, when vaccination was made compulsory for all. Smallpox disappeared.

Super soap

After 1800, cheap soap became readily available. Soap is a powerful germ-killer (although before the 1860s, people didn't know that germs caused disease).

Doctors and nurses

After 1870, doctors started to use **anaesthetics** and **antiseptics** to make operations safer and cleaner. Fewer patients died of shock, pain or infection. Nurses were better trained too. They worked in a growing number of hospitals.

Sobering up

In the 1700s, there was a craze for drinking cheap gin. Lots of **alcoholics** died as a result. Also, heavy gin drinking damaged unborn babies. In 1751, the Government put a tax on gin, making it more expensive. Fewer people were able to afford it.

Cleaner cities

After the 1860s, councils began to clean up their towns and cities. Clean water supplies and sewers were installed. Better housing was built too. The healthier towns included wider lit streets and parks for the public to use.

Baby boom

After 1800, there were more and more factories. These employed child workers. Some parents had more children knowing that they could send them out to earn money.

Clever kids

Education improved. After 1870, better schools improved **literacy**. Now people could read booklets giving advice about health, diet, cleaning, childcare and care of the sick. People began to lead healthier lives.

HUNGRY FOR MORE? *Find out the population of Britain today. Why not create a graph or chart to represent Britain's population from 1750 to today?*

! WISE UP WORDS

census   immigrants   immigration   midwives
literacy   maternity   anaesthetic   antiseptic
alcoholic

WORK

1 Write a sentence or two for each of the following words:
   immigration • census • population

2 a Copy **Source A** into your book. Remember to label it clearly.

   b Write down *at least* two observations about the information in the bar chart.

3 Make three lists. In one, write down all the factors that *increase* the number of births. In the next, write down factors that *decrease* the number of deaths. In the final list, write down factors that do both.

4 Use all you have learned to answer this essay question:

   'Why did the population 'explode' after 1750?'

   Your teacher will help you to plan it carefully. Your essay should include:

   • An introduction – facts and figures about the increase in population.

   • Paragraphs about the reasons for increased births and decreased deaths.

   • A conclusion – a summary of your findings.

HISTORY MYSTERY

Who killed Tom Carter?

In 1750, 80% of the British population lived and worked in the countryside. Families farmed small strips of land dotted all over the village and grew enough food to feed themselves. If the harvest was especially good, they might sell their **surplus** at market. After 1750, the population grew rapidly. More food was needed and the farmers had to grow it. Some families realised that if they grew more food, they could make more money. They used the latest inventions (like Jethro Tull's Seed Drill, which planted seeds in a straight line and covered them back over) to produce more food.

Other farmers bought some of their neighbours' strips of land to make bigger farms. Bigger farms meant potential for bigger profits and this process became known as 'enclosing'. Any farmers left without any land (because they'd sold it) either got work on the new **enclosed farms** or moved to the local town.

Now it is time to be a History Mystery detective. Can you piece together the clues and solve this rural riddle?

Source A is a map of Brympton Turville, a small village typical of thousands in Britain in the late 1700s. You may notice that none of the land has been enclosed yet – the land in the West Field and the North Field is still farmed in strips – the farmers of Brympton Turville didn't start enclosing the land until a few years after Tom Carter's death.

Study the map carefully. At 6:30am on 5 May 1796, the dead body of Tom Carter – a poor unemployed farmer – was found lying in a lane in the village. He'd been shot through the neck.

As a History Mystery detective, use the map and the clues in **Source B** to solve the puzzle of who killed Tom Carter. You should be able to work out what happened to Tom on the night of 4 May 1796. Good luck!

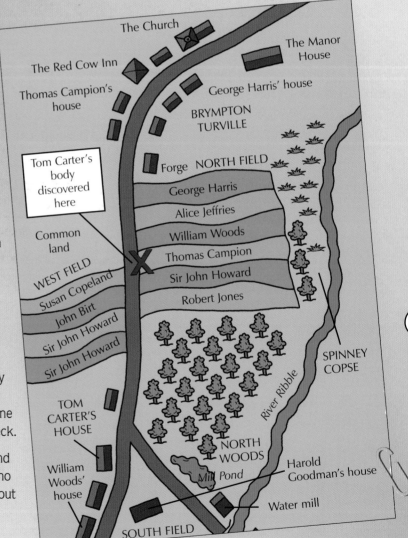

▲ **Source A** A map of Brympton Turville

 WISE UP WORDS

surplus   poaching   enclosed farms

1. Tom Carter left the Red Cow Inn at 11:30pm on 4 May.
2. Tom Carter had been unemployed since 6 March 1796. He had a wife and three children to support.
3. Sir John Howard, who owned a lot of land in the area and lived in The Manor House, had recently announced that anyone caught **poaching** on his land would be dealt with 'severely'.
4. John Chapman, who worked at the mill, had borrowed a hunting rifle from Sir John Howard on 3 May.
5. At about 11:35pm on 4 May, a shot was heard coming from Spinney Copse in North Field.
6. William Woods had been seen shooting at crows at about 8:00pm on 4 May.
7. Tom Carter had been drinking in the Red Cow Inn from about 7:30pm on 4 May.
8. Harold Smith was a very heavy drinker. On the night of 4 May, he had drunk 12 pints of cider.
9. Robert Jones had been seen with John Birt's wife recently.
10. William Woods owned one strip in North Field, none in West Field and 13 in South Field (not shown on the map).
11. Alice Jeffries hated Susannah Carter (Tom's wife). They had argued about ducks on the mill pond.
12. Tom Carter had quarrelled with Harold Smith, the village blacksmith, over the payment of drinks at the Red Cow Inn. They nearly had a fight.
13. Sir John Howard's wife, Lady Margaret, often tried to help out poorer children in the village.
14. Harold Goodman had been accused of poaching deer in 1795. No evidence was found.
15. William Woods thought Alice Jeffries was a witch.
16. Some people thought Tom Carter was having an affair with Alice Jeffries.
17. William Woods owned an old gun.
18. Robert Jones had a violent temper.
19. A deer was found caught up in bushes in North Woods on the morning of 5 May. A bullet had grazed its back.
20. John Birt and Susan Copeland had been arguing about their strips of land on 3 May.
21. Thomas Campion used to be the boyfriend of Susannah Carter before she married Tom.
22. William Woods had argued with Alice Jeffries over weeds spreading across his strip in North Field.
23. Sir John Howard owned one strip in North Field, two in West Field and 29 strips in South Field (not shown on the map).
24. Harold Goodman owned a gun.
25. A deer was seen running across North Field at about 11:40pm on 4 May.
26. Two farm workers, George Harris and Harold Goodman, were drinking in the Red Cow Inn on the night of 4 May. They left at 10:45pm.

▲ **Source B** Information file

Who Killed Tom Carter? pages based on 'British Social and Economic History: Coursework and Questions', by Simon Mason, 1990.

WORK

Time to solve the mystery if you can…

FIRST – Ignore any evidence from the information file that you think has nothing to do with Tom Carter's death. Make sure it isn't connected before you ignore it. Why don't you think it is important? Make a note of your decisions.

SECOND – Find evidence that links his death to a person.

- Who could have done it?
- How did Tom die? Think about the weapon used to kill him.
- Did anyone have a motive?
- Write down what evidence you have found.

THIRD – Remember to think about every possibility.

- Was it murder or an accident? A jury will want to know – what evidence is there for each?
- Can you back up your thoughts with evidence from the information file?
- Make a note of your findings.

FINALLY – Time to make up your mind. Who killed Tom Carter?

- Write a short paragraph outlining your theory about his death. Perhaps you could imagine you are writing a report for a local investigator or Justice of the Peace.
- Back up your theory with evidence.

Compare your theory with that of a friend, or others in your class. Do you all agree?

Why did some towns get so big?

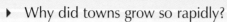

AIMS

- ▶ Why did towns grow so rapidly?
- ▶ Why were the first factories built?
- ▶ What was the impact of the steam engine?
- ▶ How does a factory 'create' a town?

Look at **Sources A** and **B**. Each source shows a view of Sheffield, one painted in 1750, the other painted 100 years later, in 1850. Study the two paintings carefully and look at how Sheffield changed.

You might want to write down some of the changes you can see or 'brainstorm' them with the person next to you.

◀ **Source A** Sheffield in 1750

You've probably noticed huge differences in the town. In **Source A**, Sheffield looks like a peaceful place, perhaps just a bit bigger than a village. The church dominates the town and seems to be in the centre of things. Fields surround Sheffield and there seems to be some farm work going on. You should be able to see cows, haystacks and perhaps horses.

By 1850, Sheffield had changed ... a lot! In **Source B**, it looks a lot dirtier, all smoky and polluted. A factory or two has appeared and the workers' houses (behind the chimney stacks) are built in rows. Can you see the railway and the canal?

◀ **Source B** Sheffield in 1850

Sheffield was typical of many towns that grew and grew during this time.

Life was slow in 1750. The horse was the fastest form of transport and, with a good clear spell, you might be able to get from London to Manchester in four days!

Although there were plenty of small towns like Sheffield, people worked on the land and lived in villages out in the countryside. In fact, in 1750, eight out of ten people lived in **rural** areas. Life was tough in these places and people produced just enough to scrape by – wheat, barley, potatoes – perhaps keeping a few animals to provide milk or eggs. A good harvest, which was always celebrated, might provide enough extra food to sell in nearby market towns. Poor harvests were deadly – if crops were ruined by bad weather, or sheep and cows were killed by disease, the consequences were devastating. People starved to death! Most families also made goods in their own homes to sell as well. Shoes, socks, buttons, lace, hats, gloves, nails, work tools and clay pots were just a few examples of the sort of items that people made in their own homes, or in workshops attached to their homes. The whole family would join in too. Mums, dads and children all had their part to play in this **domestic system** (domestic means involving the home or family).

FACT: ▶ The local town

▶ In 1750, towns were nowhere near as big as they are today; for example, the population of Leeds in 1751 was about 12 000 people.

Towns often contained the local specialists, like the blacksmith, the butcher, the baker and the candlestick maker!

Some towns were well-known for the top-quality goods the townspeople produced. Kidderminster was famous for making carpets whilst Redditch produced some of Britain's best needles.

HUNGRY FOR MORE?

As you have read, some towns specialised in producing particular goods. Find out what these ten towns were famous for making:

Nottingham • Northampton • Stoke on Trent • Grimsby • St Helens • Axminster • Norwich • High Wycombe • Birkenhead • Burton on Trent

! WISE UP WORDS

rural   domestic system

▼ **Source C** A small workshop in 1750. A few families may be working together here. Few, if any, machines were used as most goods were produced using hand-powered tools.

WORK

1 Write a sentence or two about each of the 'wise up words'.

2 a Look at **Sources A** and **B**. Make a list of some of the changes that happened to Sheffield between the years 1750 and 1850.

  b In your opinion, what was the biggest change?

  c Would you have preferred to live in the Sheffield of 1750 or 1850? Give reasons for your choice.

3 In as much detail as you can, describe what is going on in **Source C**. Use details from the picture in your answer.

4 Imagine you live in a rural area, just outside Sheffield, in 1750. Write a short letter to a friend describing your life.

One of the most common goods introduced in people's homes was woollen cloth. As the population increased, there were more people to buy it! The whole family worked together to produce loads and loads of top-quality material. The whole process worked like this:

1 A **clothier** (wool tradesman) buys the wool from the farmer.

2 The clothier takes the wool to the villagers, who turn it into cloth.

FACT: ▶ Urghh!!

▶ The family collected their urine in a tub all week (what a smell!). It was later sold for a penny a tub to the local **fuller**, who used it to bleach cloth!

3 The family could work whatever hours they wanted ... as long as they met their deadlines.

4 The clothier collects the cloth and pays the villagers for what they have produced.

He or she brings them more wool for next week's order!

5 The clothier takes the cloth to be dyed, then sold.

It wasn't just wool that was turned into cloth. The soft fibres of the cotton plant (grown in warmer places like India) were turned into thread, which was then woven into cloth. Soon, cotton cloth became more popular than woollen cloth.

Source D Cloth-making in the 1750s. Look for:

i) the woman on the right untangling the wool and straightening it. This was called **carding**.

ii) the spinner – the woman in the centre is twisting the woollen fibres into single threads on a **spinning wheel**.

iii) the man who is on the left, weaving the threads, or **yarn**, into cloth on a special machine called a **loom**.

Source E Daniel Defoe, a traveller, describes Halifax in 1726

'Men and women, and children who were hardly above four years old, were busy carding and spinning or at the loom, all so they could gain their bread.'

Many cloth merchants made their fortunes out of the cloth trade ... and they wanted to keep making money. They were helped by clever inventors who dreamed up machines to speed up the cloth-making process. In 1733, John Kay invented his **flying shuttle**, which speeded up weaving and allowed weavers to produce

more cloth. Then, in 1764, James Hargreaves invented his **spinning jenny** machine, which allowed spinners to spin more thread.

Both of these machines still allowed the cloth to be produced in homes. They were powered by people and were small enough to fit into a cottage. It was the next invention that started to change things – and it was going to encourage work in factories.

FACT: Kill Kay!

▶ Some weavers were worried that the new inventions might replace them. They were afraid of losing their jobs. One group of angry weavers took it out on John Kay. They wrecked his house and smashed his machines. Kay ended up running away to France!

! WISE UP WORDS

fuller   flying shuttle   yarn   carding   loom
clothier   spinning wheel   spinning jenny

WORK

1 a Match each word on the left with the correct description on the right.

clothier	a simple machine used to twist woollen fibres into single threads
carding	a special machine that weaves yarn into cloth
spinning wheel	the process of untangling wool
yarn	a man who buys and sells wool
loom	a man who uses urine to bleach cloth
fuller	fine threads made by twisting wool

   b Why did John Kay, inventor of the 'flying shuttle', have to move from his home in England to France?

2 You are a clothier. As the population grows, you find you are buying and selling more cloth. You have to hire an apprentice to help you with your busy work life.

• Write out a list of instructions for him or her. It should range from collecting the wool to fetching the finished cloth.

• Remember to include information and advice on what happens to the wool and the problems they might encounter.

The man most responsible for the switch from home to factory production was Richard Arkwright. In 1769, he invented his '**spinning frame**', a machine that produced thick, strong thread ... fast!

It was so big that it couldn't be used in people's homes as it had to be powered by a horse or waterwheel. Arkwright's solution was to build a factory to house his huge spinning machines. His first opened in 1771 at Cromford in Derbyshire. He soon had factories all over Britain. His ideas were copied by many other businessmen, not only in Britain, but in other countries too!

Arkwright's invention (and the amount of money he was making) inspired others to invent machines to produce cloth quicker and in greater quantities than ever before. In 1779, Samuel Crompton's **spinning mule** enabled factories to produce thread that was better quality than Arkwright's. Then, in 1787, Edmund Cartwright produced a **power loom** that speeded up weaving to the point where weavers were unable to use all that the spinners could produce.

Whilst some families continued to work at home, by 1820, most had left their villages and gone to work in the factories. The domestic system was dying out. It was being replaced by the new way to work – the **factory system**.

As the factories grew and new ones were built, the factory owners built more and more houses for their workers. Soon, the majority of British people would be living in these new towns.

- When working at home, people were used to working whenever it suited them. The factories changed all that. Now workers had to work when the factory owner told them to.
- Some workers couldn't get used to working for a 'boss' when they were used to working with their families. Factory owners were forced to introduce strict codes of discipline. In one of Arkwright's mills, one man was fired for 'being late for no reason'. Another was fired for 'terrifying S Pearson with an ugly face' and 'putting Mr Haynes' dog in a bucket of hot water'.
- The factory owners made huge profits. Arkwright bought himself a country estate and built a huge mansion.

▼ **Source F** A foreign visitor to England, 1823

'The modern factories are a miracle. They are eight or nine stories high and have 40 windows along their front. A number of these factories stand in very high positions and dominate the neighbourhood.'

- In one week, an operator working his factory machine could produce over 60 times more cloth than a whole family working at home.
- Women and children worked in the factories as well as the men. They were cheap to employ.
- Some factory owners refused to employ men unless they brought their wives and children with them.
- Water-power meant that the machines (and workers) could work non-stop.
- It was dangerous work with no safety guards or factory inspectors to check up on dangerous conditions.

▼ **Source G** A factory worker in 1800

'We used to gather potatoes before we came here. When not doing that, I used to mend fences or make baskets. We came to the factory five years ago, it's regular work you see. I work on spinning machines and my family still work with me. The wife helps a machine operator and the kids clean. Paid once a fortnight, family wage, in my pocket. Mind you, I miss the freedom. When you're your own boss, you work when you like. Now it's all clock, clock, clock...'

 WISE UP WORDS

spinning mule   factory system   power loom
spinning frame

WORK

1   Explain what is meant by the term 'factory system'.

2   To do this question you will need to look at pages 14 and 15 *as well as* these two pages.

   a   Divide your page into four columns and put these headings at the top:

   DATE • INVENTOR • MACHINE • WHAT DID IT DO?

   b   In chronological order, list the five main inventions that helped to improve cloth-making in Britain between 1733 and 1787 and complete each column.

   c   Write a paragraph explaining why you think some people hated these new machines so much.

3   Look at **Source G**.

   a   In what ways has the factory system changed this worker's life?

   b   What do you think the worker means by 'clock, clock, clock...'?

4   Write a description of one of Britain's first factories. Use the diagram to help you. Imagine you are describing it to a person who has never seen one before. Perhaps include a picture or diagram. To focus your writing even more, you must use NO MORE than 150 words.

New factories were like magnets. They pulled people from the countryside with the promise of regular work and good wages.

As factory owners started to build houses, churches, shops and inns for their workers, places that were previously tiny villages grew into large towns. Small towns became huge, overcrowded cities.

▼ **Source I** W Thompson, a writer in 1788

'About 50 years ago, there were only three main streets in Birmingham. Today, it is a crowded and extensive town. This shows, in a very striking manner, the rapid increase in industry and trade.'

By 1800, the question of power had started to fascinate factory owners. They wanted their machines to run cheaply and quickly, for 24 hours a day if possible! Most early factories used water-power – a huge waterwheel that would drive the machinery – but this form of power had its problems (see **Source J**).

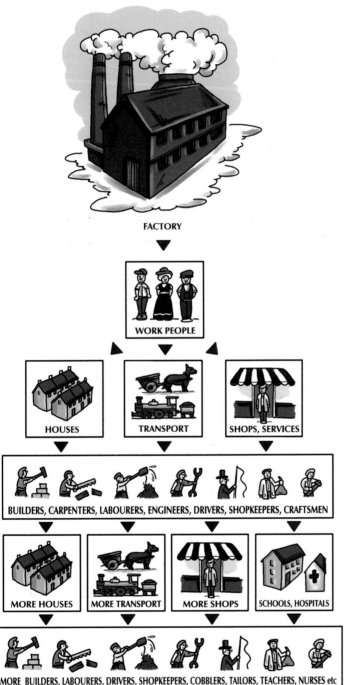

FACTORY

WORK PEOPLE

HOUSES | TRANSPORT | SHOPS, SERVICES

BUILDERS, CARPENTERS, LABOURERS, ENGINEERS, DRIVERS, SHOPKEEPERS, CRAFTSMEN

MORE HOUSES | MORE TRANSPORT | MORE SHOPS | SCHOOLS, HOSPITALS

MORE BUILDERS, LABOURERS, DRIVERS, SHOPKEEPERS, COBBLERS, TAILORS, TEACHERS, NURSES etc

▲ **Source H** How does a factory create a town?

▼ **Source J** Based on a factory owner's diary, 1805

16 December: The river is frozen. Our waterwheel will not turn and we have no power. The workers have been sent home because their looms do not function.

29 May: The hot weather has made the River Ribble very low. In the afternoons, our looms go very slow.

28 August: Work has stopped in 30 mills in Blackburn. Work will not start until it rains again.

So factory owners started to look for other ways to power their machines. Water-power just wasn't good enough. Instead, they turned to a relatively new form of power that scientists had been developing – the **steam engine**.

The first steam engines just pumped water out of mines. They were slow, expensive and kept breaking down. Then, in 1781, James Watt and his business partner, Matthew Boulton, developed a fast, reliable engine that turned a wheel. Factory owners started to take an interest when they learned that steam power could be used to drive their machinery.

steam removed here which pulls piston down

beam

piston pushed up

gears to keep wheel moving

water turned to steam

fire

wheel attached to belts which drive factory machines

Factories had not only changed the way people worked, they had also changed the places where they lived too!

▼ **Source L** George Weerth, a factory worker, 1840

'We look in astonishment as our coach drives on. The further we go, the more houses there are, collected along the road. All around we see flames, hissing and rattling. The windows of factories shaking as we go by. The sun darkens as if cloud has blocked it; suddenly it is evening on a bright day! As our horses stop, we see this is a dirty, evil-smelling town.'

! WISE UP WORDS

steam engine   industry   mechanised

▲ **Source K** How does a steam engine work? A fuel, either coal or wood, is burned, which turns water in a boiler into steam. The steam passes into the cylinder and pushes up the piston. In turn, this pushes up the beam and the beam starts to turn the wheel. Then steam is removed from the cylinder, which allows the piston to move down; the beam pulls down and the wheel keeps turning. Then it all begins again!

Steam power was much faster than water-power and it didn't depend on the weather either! This meant that factories could be built anywhere and not just near a fast flowing river. Steam-powered factories started to spring up all over Britain and attracted more workers from the countryside. Factory towns, like Birmingham, Sheffield, Manchester, Bolton and Bradford started to grow and grow. By 1850, Britain produced two-thirds of the world's cotton and two-fifths of the world's hardware (pots, pans, tools and so on), all in factories. Britain's **industry** had become **mechanised**. Further, by 1851, for the first time in history, more people were living in towns and cities than in the countryside.

WORK

1 a Copy **Source H** into your book. Remember to include a title.
  b Write a paragraph explaining the diagram.

2 Read **Source J**.

  a According to the source, what type of power is used in this factory?
  b What problems does this type of power cause the factory owner?

3 a In your own words, explain how a steam engine works. You may add a diagram to illustrate your answer.
  b What advantages does steam power have over water-power?

4 Write a sentence or two to explain the following words:

    industry • mechanised

Factory life: are you tough enough?

 AIM ▸ What was it like to work in a factory in the nineteenth century?

If you could visit one of the first factories in Britain, perhaps the first thing you would notice would be the disgusting and dangerous working conditions. Most factory owners only cared about making a profit, not wasting money on providing a safe place to work. The machines were not fitted with any safety covers or guards and workers were not provided with goggles to protect their eyes. Factories were so noisy that people often went deaf and the dust made everyone sick. These hot, sweaty places would smell as well … the stench would come from overflowing toilet buckets at the end of each room!

You would also notice a lot of children. Poor children did not go to school so boys and girls, some as young as five, would go to work with their parents. Put yourself in the position of a 14-year-old factory boy or girl in the early 1800s. They had probably been working for about seven or eight years. Look through the following information about working lives and ask yourself 'would you be tough enough to cope'?

▼ **Source B** From a modern history textbook published in the 1980s – 'History Alive 3, 1789–1914', by Peter Moss

'No one, not even small children, was allowed to sit down, except during lunch. Even during their short breakfast and tea breaks, many factories kept their engines running so that the workers had to eat with one hand and operate their looms or jennies with the other. These long hours spent hunched over the machines added stomach complaints, varicose veins and ulcers to the long list of diseases from which the workers suffered. Perhaps even worse, small children, who often had to bend their bodies in unnatural positions to do their job properly, frequently grew up with twisted spines, crooked thighs and knock-knees.'

▼ **Source C** An interview with Mr Moss, a factory supervisor, in 1816

Q: 'Were many children injured in the machinery?'
A: 'Very frequently, very often their fingers were crushed, and one had his arm broken.'
Q: 'Were any of the children deformed?'
A: 'Yes, several: there were two or three that were very crooked.'

▼ **Source A** From a report on conditions in factories made to Parliament in 1864

'Little boys and girls are seen at work at the machines and their fingers are in constant danger of being cut off. "They hardly ever lose a whole hand," said one of the owners, "it only takes off a finger at the first or second joint. They're just careless."'

▼ **Source D** This source is based on an interview with a **pauper apprentice**. These were orphan boys who worked in the factories for no wages, but were given a bed and food to eat. The factory practically owned them.

'The room was full of young boys and girls all dressed the same, in just a shirt and trousers. We didn't wear shoes or socks. Dinner was hot: boiled potatoes, bread and porridge. Sometimes we had bacon too. We didn't get any plates; instead, we just held out the bottom of our shirts and they poured in the food. We were always so hungry that we ate every last bit. Next, the hungry crew ran to tables of newcomers and ate anything they'd left.'

Inspector: Tell me boy, where do you live?
Child: 26 Duke Street, Leeds.
I: Do you work in the factories?
C: Yes Sir.
I: At what age did you begin to work in them?
C: I was nearly eight years, I think.
I: How many hours a day do you work?
C: From six in the morning until seven at night.
I: Are you beaten at work?
C: Yes Sir. If we look up from our work or speak to each other, we are beaten.
I: If you don't go as fast as the machines, are you beaten?
C: Yes Sir. There's screaming among the boys and girls all day. They make black and blue marks on our bodies.
I: Are you allowed to 'make water' any time of the day?
C: No, only when a boy comes to tell you it's your turn. Whether you want to go or not, that's the only time you're allowed to go.
I: Can you hold your water for that long?
C: No, we're forced to let it go.
I: Do you spoil and wet yourself then?
C: Yes.

▲ **Source E** An inspector's report on children in factories. What do you think is meant by the words 'make water'?

▼ **Source F** Danger! None of the machines have safety covers or guards.

▼ **Source G** A description of the accidental death of a young factory girl

'She was caught by her apron strings, which wrapped around the machine. She was repeatedly whirled around and around until she was killed. Her right leg was found some distance away from the machine.'

go to pg 74

▾ **Source H** This set of rules appeared in a factory in 1844. The **overseer** was the workers' supervisor. 6d was about half a day's pay for a woman. Children earned about half the amount of women workers. Men earned twice as much as women.

FACTORY RULES

1. Any worker late for work – 3d fine. They will not be let into the factory until breakfast time.

2. Any worker leaving the room without permission – 3d fine.

3. All broken brushes, oil cans, windows, wheels etc. will be paid for by the worker.

4. Any worker seen talking to another, heard whistling, singing or swearing – 6d fine.

5. Any worker who is ill and fails to find someone to do their job – 6d fine.

By Order of T Wright, Overseer, 1844

▾ **Source I** From a report to Parliament, 1843

'In Willenhall, West Midlands, the children are shamefully and cruelly beaten with a whip, strap, stick, hammer, handle, file or whatever tool is nearest to hand, or are struck with the clenched fist or kicked.'

▾ **Source J** From a leaflet about working conditions in 1837

'Girls loved their long hair, so they were sometimes punished by having it cut close to the head.'

▾ **Source K** An overseer about to punish a child. BEWARE: This picture appeared in a report on children's working conditions. The writer wanted Parliament to ban child labour. Some historians believe that the report, including this picture, was exaggerated to make things appear worse than they were.

PAUSE FOR THOUGHT

*How did the painter of **Source K** make the factory seem a very sad and cruel place?*

Why might this artist have been trying to make the factory seem worse than it really was?

▼ **Source L** A typical working day in a factory in about 1820, Monday to Saturday. A Sunday was a 'short' day of four hours' work – cleaning the machinery was a common Sunday task.

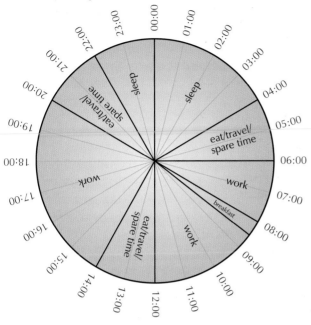

▼ **Source M** A report written by a visitor to a mill in Bolton, 1844

'The factory folk were better clothed, better fed and better educated than many other people. The factory was very clean. The working rooms were spacious, well ventilated and lofty, kept at an even temperature and clean. I observed great care in the boxing up of dangerous machinery and was told that accidents were very rare.'

FACT: ▶ You're late

▶ Some greedy factory owners moved all the factory clocks forward by 15 minutes in the morning, so all the factory workers arrived late. They were fined! By evening, the clocks had been put 15 minutes back, so the owners could get extra work without paying the workers for it!

WISE UP WORDS

overseer   deformed   pauper apprentice

WORK

1   Write a sentence or two to explain the following words:

overseer • pauper apprentice

2   Study **Source L**.

a   Make your own 24-hour pie chart for a typical day in *your* life (choose a week day). Be careful to include:

- all your sleep time
- the times for eating, travelling, breaks and any spare time
- what work you do (a paper round perhaps)

NOTE: You will also have to include something that a 14-year-old factory boy or girl wouldn't do … school!

b   Write at least five sentences, each one stating how your day is different (or similar) to a child's in 1820.

c   Why do you think the treatment of children in Britain has changed so much? Explain your answer carefully – you are being asked for your opinion here.

3   Read **Source M**.

a   In what ways is this source different to most of the others?

b   Can you think of any reasons why this factory could have been different?

4   Imagine you have been given the job of carrying out a factory inspection. Write a report for the Government based on the information on pages 20 to 23.

Include sections on:

- Dangerous and unhealthy conditions – What accidents have you heard about? Why are some children deformed? What diseases and illnesses do workers catch?
- Cruelty and punishments – How are rule breakers treated? Are punishments appropriate?
- The future – Why do some owners seem unwilling to make their factories safer? What improvements could be made?

Perhaps you could include an interview in your report (with a factory owner and/or a worker) and a picture or diagram to illustrate your points.

TOP TIP:

Be aware that <u>all</u> factories were <u>not</u> the same
– see **Source M**.

'It is one of the wonders of the world...'

AIMS
- ▶ What was special about Abraham Darby III's bridge?
- ▶ How was iron made and why did it become so popular?

In 1784, John Byng wrote that a certain bridge in Shropshire was 'one of the wonders of the world'. So special was this bridge that copies of it were made in Paris and Berlin. Many foreigners came to see it. One visitor even travelled from Australia to walk over it ... and it took him months to get to Britain by ship! But why was this bridge so special? Why did people travel from all over the world just to stare at it? And what did the bridge show about the special qualities of the new 'wonder material' it was made from?

▲ **Source A** The bridge, painted by William Williams in 1780

The most observant amongst you may have noticed that the bridge was not made from stone or wood. It was, in fact, made from iron. In the 1780s, iron was becoming more and more popular.

The increasing population was keen to buy such objects as iron cooking pots, iron pans, iron beds and iron gates. They worked in factories using iron machines that were driven by iron steam engines. Even the factories themselves used iron beams and pillars to make the buildings strong.

▼ **Source B** How to make iron in the 1700s

❶

Iron ore is dug from the ground.

❷

Iron ore is then melted, together with limestone and coke (coal that has been heated) in a furnace. Hot liquid iron pours out of the iron ore.

❸

Hot liquid iron is poured into a cast and then used for pots, pans, pipes and beams (but can be quite brittle though).

❹

When **cast iron** is reheated and hammered, it produces a purer, tougher, 'bendier' iron called **wrought iron**. This is then used for nails, chains, tools, furniture, ornaments and so on.

By the late 1780s, some iron makers were making a fortune. The Darby family based in Coalbrookdale, Shropshire, had been making top-quality iron for many years. The owner of the **ironworks**, Abraham Darby III (his father and grandfather, both called Abraham, owned the company before him), was keen to show the world how good his iron was. His solution was to build the world's first iron bridge, over the River Severn at Coalbrookdale, then one of Europe's busiest rivers. People thought he was mad – they said that the iron would never be strong enough to hold the carts and the carriages passing over his bridge.

Work started in November 1777 and took four years. At a cost of over £6 000 – a fortune then – the world's first iron bridge opened on New Year's Day, 1781. It immediately caused a sensation. Writers and artists came from all over the world to see it. Descriptions of the bridge appeared in novels and pictures appeared on pottery, clocks and furniture. Thomas Jefferson, soon to be the third President of the USA, even bought pictures of the bridge from the French in 1786.

FACT: ▶ No free tickets

▸ Darby charged EVERYONE to use his bridge. Even walking over it cost a small fee. He caused outrage when he put up a sign stating that the bridge was his private property and 'every officer or soldier, whether on duty or not, is liable to pay ... as well as the Royal Family'. That's right, he charged the King for using it!

▾ **Source C** Iron produced in Britain 1750–1900. After 1856, steel (made from iron) started to be produced in Britain too.

Year	How much was produced in Britain?
1750	30 000 tons
1800	250 000 tons
1850	2 000 000 tons
1900	6 000 000 tons

▾ **Source D** From a modern history textbook, 'Investigating History, Britain 1750–1900', by John D Clare

'People in Britain went iron mad ... the army used iron for cannon; the navy used it for ships. The new factories were made of iron and so were the machines that were used in them. Iron was used for trains and tools. In the home, it was used for fireplaces and cookers.'

FACT: ▶ Iron mad

▸ John 'Iron Mad' Wilkinson loved to find new uses for iron. He built the first iron boat in 1787, built an iron church for his workers and was even buried in an iron coffin under an iron headstone.

The Iron Bridge was a huge advertisement for iron. Railways, locomotives, buildings, machinery, cranes and ships could be made from this new, versatile 'wonder material'. Indeed, iron making became one of Britain's most important industries (see **Source C**) and people started to give the period a nickname: 'the Age of Iron'.

WISE UP WORDS

cast iron   wrought iron   ironworks

WORK

1 a In your own words, explain how iron was made.

   b What is the difference between cast iron and wrought iron?

2 Copy and complete the following paragraphs:

   After the 1780s, iron became more and more _____. It was known as the new '_____ material' because it could be used to make so many things. One iron maker, called John '_____ _____' Wilkinson, built an iron _____ for his workers and was buried in an iron _____!

   But one family emerged as the most famous iron makers of all. The _____ family, from _____ in Shropshire, owned one of the finest _____ in the world. One member of the family was so keen to show people how good his iron was, he built the world's first _____ _____ over the River _____.

3 Abraham Darby III was keen for as many people as possible to use his bridge. Pretend you work for the Darby family. Your job is to design a poster advertising their iron bridge. Include:

   • A catchy headline, for example, 'Come and visit one of the wonders of the world'.

   • Facts and figures – How much was it to build? How long did it take? Where is it?

25

Working down a mine: are you tough enough?

► Why was so much coal needed?
► What was it like to work in a mine?

Coal is a hard, black rock that is found underground. Once lit, it burns for a long time, much longer than wood. In 1750, Britain had a lot of coal in many areas and it was used mainly to heat houses and cook with. The workers that got the coal out of the ground – **miners** – didn't have to dig very deep to get at it at first. They got all they needed from large pits near the surface.

▼ **Source A** The coalfields of Britain in 1800

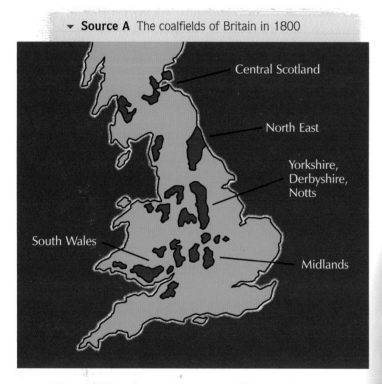

Central Scotland

North East

Yorkshire, Derbyshire, Notts

South Wales

Midlands

'Choke damp' is a poisonous gas found deep underground. It is mostly carbon dioxide.

Eight candles were collected at the bottom of the mine. One candle burns in an hour so when eight have gone, you know it's time to go home. Some men carry lamps too.

Canaries were taken underground because they stop singing when 'choke damp' is in the air. Then it was time to get out.

To dig out the coal.

Bread and cheese carried in a snap tin.

To protect elbows and knees. Made from leather – it was thick and tough.

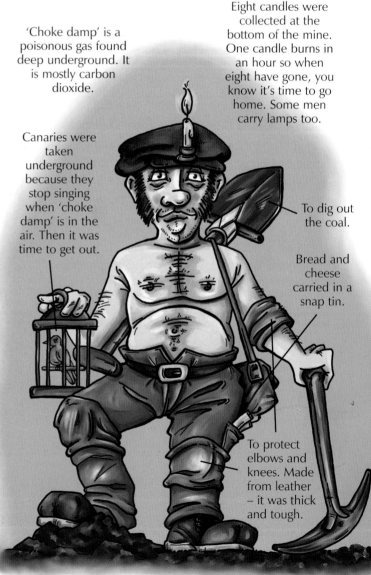

After 1750, more coal was needed ... much, much more! There were more people with homes to heat and food to cook for a start. Coal also powered steam engines in factories. It was used in the making of bricks, pottery, glass, beer, sugar, soap and, of course, iron. Coal powered steam trains across the country and steam ships across the seas. The need for more coal meant more money for the mine owners. They knew that the miners would have to dig deeper and deeper underground to get at the coal ... and this meant DANGER! Would you be tough enough to work in a mine in the 1800s?

Ready for work

Read the following interview carefully. It outlines a typical day for Daniel Douglas, a 15-year-old boy in a Durham mine.

14 August 1839

'What a day! I'm on the night shift this week, so I have to get to the cage at six in the evening. This mine is one of the deepest around here - 500 metres - but the drop to the bottom only takes about half a minute. The trip in the lift is dark, noisy and very scary. We drop about 30 metres every second and my eardrums always feel like they're going to burst. I hold on really tight because I don't want to fall out.'

'Having said goodbye to fresh air and daylight for the next ten hours, I start to "walk out". The four-mile walk to the **coalface** takes forever. By the time I actually start working, I've been down the pit for over an hour!'

'After hanging up my safety lamp (it burns brighter if there's any poisonous gas about), I light a candle for a bit of extra glow and start to dig. Using my pick and shovel, chisels and hammers, I knock out lumps of coal from the seam. The coal lies in these seams, or layers, between ordinary rock, and it's my job to pull out the coal and throw it into a large, strong sack. Young girls called **bearers** take our sacks away from the coalface and put the lumps of coal into wagons. For all of us in the mines, this job is like torture - swollen knees, bruised ribs, broken fingers and bleeding heads. The coal dust makes us cough and vomit. We do manage to eat down here but it never tastes very nice.'

'The only things that ever make us smile are the canaries, chirping away in their cages. We just keep our fingers crossed that they don't stop singing! We don't like to talk about accidents ... but we all know people who've been killed down here. Floods, roof-falls, explosions and poisonous gas claim the lives of dozens every year.'

'After eight hours of hot, dirty work on my knees, it's time to make my way back up to the surface. I always have a chat with some of the **trappers** on my way out because it was the job I used to do when I first started working here ten years ago. Those little children open and close trapdoors to let the coal wagons pass by on the underground tracks. **Drawers** push and pull the loaded wagons towards the lifts that take them up to the surface.'

'When they're not taking any coal up, the lifts take us back up to the surface - about 11 hours after I first started! Like I said, I'm working the night shift this week so it's daylight when I finish work. The mine never closes - 24 hours a day it runs - and it must be making the owner a fortune. No wonder they've started to call coal "black gold".'

'Before I collapse into bed, I check on my pigeons (I race them you see), have a cup of tea and a bite to eat before falling into a very deep sleep. I'll be back at the lift later this evening when it all starts over again.'

FACT: ▶ What a stink!

▸ Instead of lamps or candles, some miners used rotten fish for light. It glowed in the dark!

As you will have worked out, working down a mine could be a very risky business. The hours were long, the pay was low (although better than in some factories) and the conditions were very, very harsh. Most mine owners thought only about making as much money as possible so they rarely spent any money on safety measures. There were many terrible accidents and it is little wonder that miners had a lower life expectancy than most other workers!

Arthritis and **rheumatism** caused painful swelling and stiffness in muscles and joints, and was caused by years of crawling around on knees and elbows in damp conditions.

▼ **Source B** Causes of death in a Yorkshire mine, 1805

Causes of Death	Age		
	Under 13	13–18	18+
Gas explosion	12	21	43
Gunpowder explosion	1	0	1
Crushed	0	0	3
Suffocated (by choke damp)	3	0	8
Drowned	8	3	9
Hit by falling coal, stones and rubbish	23	20	55
Fall from the shafts	7	15	35
Fall from the rope breaking	0	2	3
Fall when ascending	2	2	6
Hit by wagons	5	3	9
Drawn over the pulley	5	2	3
Injuries in coal mines (unspecified)	10	6	25
Total	**76**	**74**	**200**

But accidents didn't always kill. Losing fingers, hands or feet in rock falls was common and miners often suffered from a variety of illnesses.

Black lung was the nickname given to severe coughing fits. Years and years of fine, black dust would collect in a miner's lungs leaving him short of breath and constantly coughing up black mucus.

Nystagmus was an eye illness caused by years of straining to see in poor light. It made miners' eyes very sore and they would find it difficult to focus.

▼ **Source C** A modern historian describes a miner's life, from Peter Moss' 'History Alive 3, 1789–1914'

'Because of the water, the filth and the heat, men, women and children often worked stark naked in the slushy, black mud in the dark tunnels. It is little wonder that they lived like animals below ground, and often little better when they reached the surface ... working 12 or more hours under the ground, and going down before dawn and coming up after dark, many saw daylight only on Sunday.'

▼ **Source D** Coal production, 1700–1900

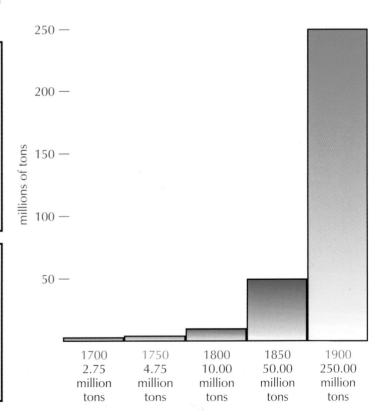

millions of tons

| 1700 2.75 million tons | 1750 4.75 million tons | 1800 10.00 million tons | 1850 50.00 million tons | 1900 250.00 million tons |

There were over 1000 deaths down the mines every year. It was such a dangerous job that in Scotland, some criminals who were sentenced to death were offered the choice of execution ... or working down the coal mines!

Yet these coal mines made lots and lots of money for their owners as they produced more and more coal. Eventually though, the Government started to take notice of all the accidents. A report on conditions in the mines was published in 1842 and the information, interviews and pictures shocked the nation. The mine owners didn't want the Government to interfere with the way they ran their mines as this might have affected their profits. However, the evidence from the 1842 Mines Report was overwhelming – perhaps the Government would soon start to pass laws to protect the miners!

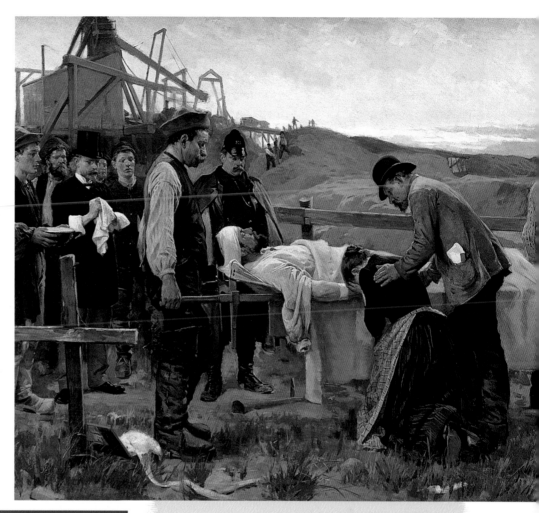

▲ **Source E** A painting called The Wounded Workman. Can you see:

i) his tearful wife?

ii) the grave crosses of dead workers?

WISE UP WORDS

coalface   black lung   miners
nystagmus   bearers   arthritis   trappers
rheumatism   drawers

WORK

1 a After 1750, why were deeper mines needed?

  b List all the dangers involved in mining. You should be able to find at least eight on pages 26 to 29.

  c Look at **Source E**. Write down at least three words or phrases to describe this famous painting. Explain why you have chosen the words.

2 Read Daniel Douglas' diary carefully.

  a At what age did he begin working down the mine?

  b Explain carefully what Daniel used to do when he first started to work in the mine.

  c What did bearers and drawers do?

  d Why might Daniel be able to see daylight when he was trying to get to sleep after work?

  e According to Daniel, why is the mine owner making so much money?

3 a Why do you think the Mines Report of 1842 shocked the nation?

  b Why do you think some mine owners didn't want the Government to interfere in their business? Explain your answer carefully.

  c Imagine you are a Member of Parliament in 1842. You are part of the investigation team who wrote the Mines Report. You want to get some changes introduced and decide to hold a public meeting to gain support.

  i) design a poster to advertise the meeting;

  ii) write out a brief speech you could make.

Turnpike fever

AIMS
▸ What was Britain's transport system like in 1750?
▸ How were roads improved?

Take two important cities: London and Edinburgh. They are about 420 miles apart. In 1750, the journey from one city to the other took a week by boat and about two weeks by road.

By 1900, the quickest journey between the two cities took nine hours. How was this improvement possible? Why had travel times reduced so much?

In 1750, getting around the country was a slow process! Coal had to get from the mines to the factories to power the machines. It had to be taken to the towns to be used as fuel to heat homes. Cotton had to move from ports to factories in order to be made into clothes. Lots of goods, like pottery, glass, soap, rugs, pots and pans all had to get to towns to be sold at market or in shops. A fast, reliable postal service was needed for businessmen too. But in 1750, there were only two ways of moving goods around the country – by water or by road – and neither of these methods were very reliable!

Using the sea or rivers was one of the cheapest ways to transport goods and it was especially useful for heavy goods, such as coal or iron. From 1750, inland rivers were being deepened or straightened so that bigger boats could use them. But there were still lots of problems with water transport. The sea could get very rough … and not all towns were near the sea. Rivers could dry up in the summer and freeze over in winter – not very helpful if you wanted some coal to heat your home on a cold wintry night! And rivers do not run all over Britain – dozens of towns were over 20 miles from their nearest river!

So the alternative to water was road transport, but roads had a host of problems too!

▾ **Source A** Written by Arthur Young, a traveller

'Let me warn all travellers … to avoid this road like the devil. They will meet here with ruts, which actually measured four feet deep and floating with mud in the summer. What can it be like in winter? I passed three carts broken down in 18 miles.'

▾ **Source B** Highway robbery was very common. Highwaymen, like the famous Dick Turpin, made travelling around a very risky business.

WANTED

Richard 'Dick' Turpin
Highwayman and murderer
Age 30 **Height** 5'9"

Born Thaxted, Essex
- he has a thin face, broad shoulders, smallpox scars
- a butcher by trade
- responsible for making it dangerous for travellers to pass over Blackheath
- did cruelly murder Thomas Morris of Epping Forest

A reward of £200 for any person who can catch him so he can be tried and convicted

▼ **Source C** From a history textbook, 'In Search of History, 1714–1900' by J F Aylett

'Each local parish [area with its own church] was supposed to look after its own roads; each villager worked for six days every year, repairing them. But the villagers hardly used the main roads. So they weren't very worried about what they were like.'

The Government eventually became tired of the rotten roads and decided to act. They divided Britain's main roads into lots of lengths of a few kilometres and rented each section to a '**turnpike trust**'. These trusts promised to improve their stretch of road and keep it in good order. In return, the trusts were allowed to charge a **toll** to road users. Turnpike roads, as they became known, had gates at the end of each stretch of road where **toll keepers** collected the money.

Some turnpike trusts employed specialist road builders to build some of the finest roads the country had ever seen.

▼ **Source D** Thomas Telford and John McAdam were two of the most famous road builders. McAdam's roads were probably the most popular (they were cheaper) and hundreds of trusts paid for 'McAdamised' roads. Years later, when **tar** was added, people called the surface 'tarmac'.

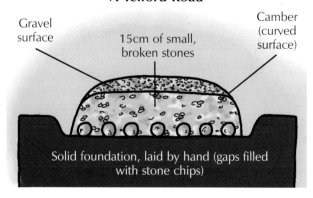

A Telford Road

Gravel surface
15cm of small, broken stones
Camber (curved surface)
Solid foundation, laid by hand (gaps filled with stone chips)

A McAdam Road

15cm of granite chippings
Camber
Road raised above ground level
2 layers of small, rough stones at bottom

By 1830, there were nearly 1 000 turnpike trusts, each trying to improve their stretch of road and make a profit at the same time. Some people called it 'turnpike fever'. These trusts controlled over 20 000 miles of road – but did the speed of transport increase very much?

The answer is quite a simple one. In 1750, it took nearly two weeks to travel from London to Edinburgh by road. By 1830, the same journey would take about 48 hours!

WISE UP WORDS

ruts   toll keepers   turnpike trust   tar   toll

WORK

1 a How long did it take to get from London to Edinburgh *by road* in 1750?

   b Why do you think it took so long? Explain your answer carefully, referring to **Sources A**, **B** and **C** as you do.

   c Why was water transport also unreliable?

2 a Match up the names on the left with the correct descriptions on the right.

   turnpike trust — a small fee or tax paid for using the road

   turnpike road — a group of businessmen, responsible for improving a stretch of road and keeping it in good order

   toll — the person who collects the tolls at the beginning of the journey

   toll keeper — a road controlled by a turnpike trust

   b Read this list of people:

   farmers • factory owners • businessmen
   pizza delivery boys • the army • tramps
   horse and coach companies

   Decide which groups gained by having better roads. In each case, give reasons why they benefited.

3 a Copy **Source D** into your book.

   b In what ways are these roads better than the road in **Source A**?

   c By 1830, how long did it take to get from London to Edinburgh?

What was 'canal mania'?

AIMS
▶ Why were roads not ideally suited to all businessmen?
▶ Why was the Bridgewater Canal built?

Although turnpike trusts built miles of top-quality roads, they still weren't suitable for some businesses. They were much too bumpy for Josiah Wedgwood, a pottery maker from Stoke. He was making thousands of teacups, saucers and teapots because tea drinking was so popular. Yet he wasn't making as much money as he could have been because his goods were being smashed on journeys along the still-too-bumpy turnpike roads. Another businessman, the Duke of Bridgewater, tried to use roads to take coal from his mines in Worsley, seven miles up the road, to sell in Manchester. But the roads were too slow and the local turnpike trust kept charging too much for his carts to use their road. Wedgwood, Bridgewater and other businessmen like them needed a solution.

It was Bridgewater who first came up with an idea. Using a brilliant engineer who worked for Wedgwood, he decided he would have a **canal** built. Its success started a period of canal building so hectic that historians have called it 'canal mania'.

The Duke wanted to get coal from his mines in Worsley to Manchester. He could take it by road, but it was too bulky and expensive.

He decided to build a canal … and borrowed a fortune to fund it.

The Duke hired a brilliant engineer to build it for him – James Brindley. He'd built many things before, but never a canal.

A canal is a long, narrow, man-made channel of water. The Bridgewater Canal was seven miles long. Barges, pulled by horses, could carry more coal than wagons on the road. They were quicker too.

Using a system of locks, canal barges could even go up and down hills or slopes. Locks are boxes with gates. The boxes can be filled or emptied with water to lower or raise the barge to different levels of the canal.

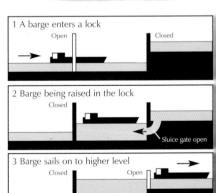

1 A barge enters a lock
Open   Closed

2 Barge being raised in the lock
Closed
Sluice gate open

3 Barge sails on to higher level
Closed   Open

Map:
N
0 km   10
scale
St. Helens
Manchester
Worsley
River Irwell
Liverpool
River Mersey

! **WISE UP WORDS**
navvies   aqueduct   canal mania   canal

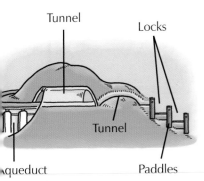

Tunnel
Locks
Tunnel
aqueduct
Paddles

The Bridgewater Canal was carried over the River Irwell on an **aqueduct**, the first in Britain. One writer said it was the 'most extraordinary thing in the Kingdom, if not in Europe'.

By 1830, it was possible to carry goods on a barge from London, through Leicester, Nottingham, Leeds, Liverpool, Birmingham, Bristol and then across England back to London again. They were ideal for carrying heavy, bulky goods, such as coal, and breakable goods like pottery. They even provided work for thousands of men (or **navvies** as they were known) who built them.

I'm making £100 000 per year!

The Bridgewater Canal was opened in 1761. It was an immediate success. The Duke's coal got to Manchester twice as fast and for half the price of road travel.

This lot would have been smashed on the bumpy roads!

Many other businessmen now wanted a canal. Brindley built more, including one for his old boss, Josiah Wedgwood. The Grand Trunk Canal opened in 1777. It brought clay to Wedgwood's potteries in Stoke and took his finished pottery to his customers.

▼ **Source A** A writer describing the Grand Trunk Canal in 1790

'The most common produce of Manchester, Birmingham and Wolverhampton — cheese, salt, lime, stone, timber, corn, paper and brick — were carried along the canal to the people of London. In return, groceries, cotton, tin, manure and other goods constantly travelled back.'

But the great age of canal building did not last long. They were still too slow for mail (fast mail coaches on roads could carry post quicker) and they could freeze up in winter or dry out in summer. There wasn't really any passenger service on the canals either. Anyway, by the 1830s, a new form of transport was hitting the headlines – the railways had arrived!

'Canal mania' started as other canal builders joined the craze. By 1830, nearly 4 000 miles of canal had been built.

WORK

1 a Draw this puzzle in your book and fill in the answers to the clues:

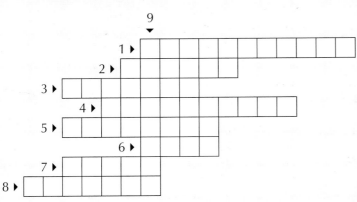

Clues:

1 It was his idea
2 The canal needed to go over this river
3 Men employed to build the canals
4 Coal was needed here
5 This carried the canal over the river
6 A way of allowing a canal to go up and down hills
7 Wedgwood made pottery here
8 Where the coal mines were

b Read *down* the puzzle (clue 9). Write a sentence about this person.

2 Use all the information on these two pages:
  a Make a list of all the reasons why roads were not suitable for some people.
  b Make another list of reasons why canals were useful to Bridgewater, Wedgwood and other businessmen.
  c Make a final list which shows some of the problems associated with canals.

3 What do you think the phrase 'canal mania' means? Explain your answer fully.

The railway age

AIMS

▸ How and why did steam **locomotives** develop?
▸ What impact did Richard Trevithick and George Stephenson have on the railway age?

When steam engines first appeared in the 1700s, inventors wondered whether steam power could be used for turning wheels. If it could, surely the invention of the locomotive – a steam engine that moved wheels along a set of rails – was not far away. By 1800, the race was on to build a safe and reliable steam locomotive.

The man credited with building the world's first railway locomotive is a Cornishman called Richard Trevithick. In 1804, to win a bet, his engine pulled ten tons of iron and 70 passengers for nine miles in Merthyr Tydfil, South Wales. The journey took four hours and many at the time said it would have been quicker if they had walked! Nevertheless, it was a historic journey.

Four years later, he raced his new locomotive – Catch Me Who Can – against horses on a round track on the site of what is now Euston Station in London. He charged passengers 5p for a ride.

▾ **Source A** The Catch Me Who Can of 1808. Trevithick was a clever engineer, but not a good businessman. He died a poor man in 1833.

Other engineers saw their chance to make money. One of them was George Stephenson, who built his first locomotive – the Blucher – in 1814. It pulled coal (very slowly) at his local mine, Killingworth Colliery.

In 1821, Stephenson was asked to build a 20-mile rail track from the port of Stockton on Tees to a coal mine in Darlington. The owner of the mine, Edward Pease, intended to use horses to pull carts full of coal along the track, but Stephenson persuaded him to use one of his steam locomotives instead. On 27 September 1825, Stephenson's Locomotion pulled 12 wagons full of coal, a coach and 21 passenger cars at the opening of the Stockton to Darlington Railway. This was the first public transport system in the world to use steam locomotives. Some passengers fainted when the train reached the speed of 12 miles per hour – they were absolutely terrified!

A year later, Stephenson was given a much bigger job. He was asked to plan and build the first railway line between major cities: Liverpool and Manchester. The railway would run for 30 miles, include a huge tunnel, 63 bridges and a **viaduct** to carry the railway over a river. He also had to get through Chat Moss, a large area of marshland. By 1829, Stephenson had solved all the engineering problems and the line was nearing completion.

In October 1829, a contest was arranged at Rainhill, just outside Liverpool, to see if any engineer could design a safe and reliable engine to use on the new railway. Four men entered their locomotives, including Stephenson with his engine called the Rocket.

 WISE UP WORDS

locomotive   viaduct

A huge crowd turned up to watch the contestants race their engines on a two-mile length of track. As well as Stephenson, the owners of three other engines – the Sanspareil, the Novelty and the Perseverance – were all keen to get their hands on the £500 prize.

▼ **Source B** The Rocket

▼ **Source C** Based on a letter written by one of Stephenson's assistants after the contest

16 October 1829

'Dear James

We have just finished the contest and the *Rocket* has been triumphant. We will take hold of the £500. The *Rocket* is the best engine I have ever seen.

The *Sanspareil* burns a lot of fuel and mumbles and roars and rolls about like an empty beer barrel on a rough pavement. She is very ugly too. The *Novelty* seemed to dart away like a greyhound for a bit but wasn't reliable – always something exploding or blowing up. The *Perseverance* was last of all to start and was slow and noisy – as noisy as a pair of wicker baskets on an old donkey!'

The Rocket won easily and reached speeds of 30 miles per hour. A year later, on 15 September 1830, the Rocket was being used at the opening ceremony of the Liverpool to Manchester Railway. By December, dozens of trains were carrying passengers, coal, timber, cattle, sheep and pigs between the two cities. By 1831, the railway was taking over £200 000 each year in fares. And it was only taking just over an hour to get from Liverpool to Manchester, much faster than road or canal. Without a doubt, the 'railway age' had begun.

▼ **Source D** A picture of the opening of the Liverpool to Manchester Railway, 1830

WORK

1 Explain what is meant by the word 'locomotive'.

2 Each of these dates is important in railway history:

   1814 • 1825 • 1804 • 1830 • 1821 • 1826 • 1808 • 1829

   a Put the dates in chronological order on separate lines in your book.
   b Beside each date, write what happened in that year in your own words.

3 Read **Source C**.

   a Why were the Rainhill Trials taking place?
   b According to this source, why did the *Rocket* win the trial?
   c Why do you think the *Rocket* and lots of important famous people (like the Prime Minister) were asked to be at the opening of the Liverpool to Manchester Railway?
   d Was the opening day a success or not? Give reasons for your answer.

How did railways change people's lives?

AIMS
▸ What impact did the railways have on industry?
▸ What impact did the railways have on ordinary people?
▸ How did the railways reduce travel time?

The building of the railways in Britain changed many things: some of these changes were huge; others were smaller and apparently insignificant but still made a difference to people's lives.

By 1850, just 20 years after the opening of the first city-to-city line, there were over 7 000 miles of track linking London to nearly all the major towns and cities of Britain (see **Source A**).

Trains were three times faster than even the fastest coach on the road and eight times faster than canal barges. They could carry a lot more too and they were cheap – much cheaper than the turnpike roads, but still not as cheap as the canals. But businessmen were prepared to pay that bit extra to get their goods across the country that much quicker. They didn't want to lose orders because a buyer was left waiting for a delivery of cotton shirts, leather shoes, coal or china teapots! So it wasn't long before canal companies and turnpike trusts were going bankrupt – the railways had simply taken all their business.

The railways themselves created work too. Iron, steel, bricks and timber were needed to build all the things associated with railways – locomotives, trucks, carriages, rails, sleepers, signals, buildings and much more. Coal was needed in huge quantities for the locomotives: a journey of 100 miles used about one ton of coal. Men were needed as rail workers too – guards, drivers, mechanics, maintenance and so on. It has been estimated that by 1880, about 300 000 jobs were connected in some way to the railways. Even whole new 'railway' towns emerged where different sections of track all joined up. In 1841, Crewe was a village of 203 people: by 1871, it had grown to 18 000 people and was a major railway town.

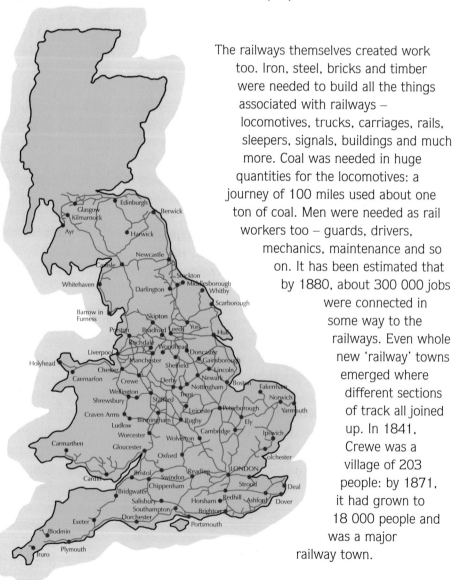

▲ **Source A** The railway network in 1852. Some of the great engineers of the day – George and Robert Stephenson and Isambard Kingdom Brunel – planned and built some of the railway network.

▲ **Source B** The Railway Station (1862), a painting by William Frith. Look out for: i) a thief being arrested ii) a recently married couple   iii) a boy off to boarding school   iv) a soldier saying goodbye (or hello) to his child

During the 1840s, Thomas Cook began organising cheap day train trips to the seaside. Overnight, he invented the great British tradition of the 'day at the seaside'. Towns such as Blackpool and Margate all grew as a direct result of the railways. Hotels, cafes, piers, funfairs and theatres were all built for holidaymakers.

Special trains took passengers to race meetings, cricket matches and football games too. Now football teams could travel 'away' to play games against each other. The national football league, which began in 1888 with 12 teams, could never have started without the railways.

The food industry also grew as a result of the railways. Foods such as milk, vegetables, meat and fish could be taken into cities and towns while it was still fresh. Farmers started to enjoy bigger incomes as a result of the railway age.

There were other public benefits too. The mail speeded up, national newspapers could be read on the same day in different parts of Britain, theatre companies toured the country and every morning people began to tell the same time. Before the railways, people operated on local time – clocks in Reading were four minutes ahead of those in London, while the time in Bristol was 11 minutes behind! The railways couldn't run lots of different timetables in many different time zones, so in 1852, the whole country adopted Greenwich Mean Time – and the timetable made sense.

By 1900, there were over 20 000 miles of train track carrying millions of passengers every year. London even had its own underground railway that workers used to travel into the City from the growing suburbs. And the journey time! Our original journey between London and Edinburgh took two weeks in 1750. By 1900, it would have taken nine hours – thanks to the railway!

WORK

Your task is to produce an extended piece of writing that answers the question, 'What was the impact of the railways on Britain?'

FIRST: Plan the content.
  a Produce a spider diagram listing all the changes that the railways brought. Write a sentence about each change.
  b Start to put these changes into categories:
     i) speed of travel ii) creating jobs iii) 'days out' iv) food v) any other changes

SECOND: Draft out your essay. Your teacher should be able to help you with a few 'sentence starters' or a writing frame.

THIRD: Check your draft copy carefully and copy it out into your book.

3 • An age of invention

The National Awards for Invention and Design, 1750–1900

AIMS

▸ Who were the great designers, inventors and scientists between 1750 and 1900?
▸ How did their inventions improve life for the British?

Between 1750 and 1900, the British were a very inventive lot! They designed new ways to do things that no one had ever thought of before. New machines did things better, faster and for longer. Then they were redesigned and further improved. Some of Britain's greatest inventors and designers lived during this time and, as a result, Britain's technology became the envy of the world. You've got six candidates to choose from, each one an important figure in Britain's gradual emergence as the 'workshop of the world' and the 'hotbed of invention'. Now it's up to you to decide who was the most important figure during this time.

> **TOP TIP!**
> For each entrant think – Why were they important?
> How did they change things?
> Are they more important than any other?

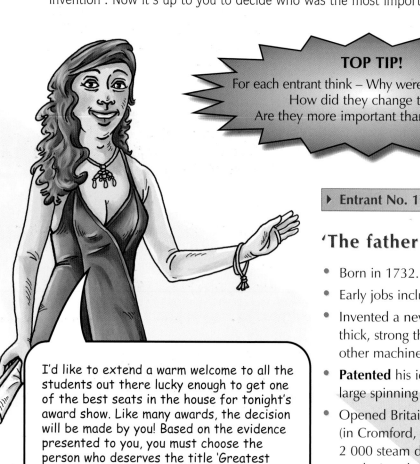

I'd like to extend a warm welcome to all the students out there lucky enough to get one of the best seats in the house for tonight's award show. Like many awards, the decision will be made by you! Based on the evidence presented to you, you must choose the person who deserves the title 'Greatest Inventor and/or Designer, 1750–1900'.

▸ **Entrant No. 1: Richard Arkwright**

'The father of the factory system'

- Born in 1732.
- Early jobs included hairdressing and wig making.
- Invented a new spinning machine that could make thick, strong thread very fast, much faster than any other machine.
- **Patented** his idea and built factories to house these large spinning machines.
- Opened Britain's first steam-powered cotton factory (in Cromford, Derbyshire). By 1813, there were over 2 000 steam driven spinning machines in Britain producing cloth worth £40 million! To some, he was 'the father of the factory system'.
- Opened lots of factories, employing thousands of people.
- After being knighted in 1786, he still felt he wasn't clever enough to be worthy of the title 'Sir Richard'. He sat down every day to improve his reading, writing and spelling.

▶ **Supporter No. 1:** The modern historians, Paul Shuter and John Child, in 'The Changing Face of Britain'

'Richard Arkwright … was certainly a great entrepreneur. He had faith in the inventions, he risked his money and persuaded other people to risk theirs. He got very rich in the process… Without the inventors, industry as we know it could not have started. Without entrepreneurs, it could not have developed. They decided which risks to take. When they were successful, they laid the foundations for our industry today.'

▶ **Supporter No. 2:** The modern historian, J F Aylett, from 'In Search of History, 1714–1900'

'But Arkwright was a clever businessman … in the mill; thousands of spindles were all spinning thread at once. By his death [in 1792] Arkwright was running ten mills; he had made himself a fortune of £500 000. And the factory age had arrived.'

▲ **Source A** One of Arkwright's spinning machines, often called a 'water frame' because his first factories used waterwheels to drive the machines before converting to steam power.

▶ **Entrant No. 2: Isambard Kingdom Brunel**

'A master engineer'

- Born in 1806, the son of Marc Brunel, the first man to build a tunnel under the River Thames.
- At 23, he designed the Clifton Suspension Bridge in Bristol. He once worked for 96 hours without a break!

- In 1833, he designed and built the Great Western Railway, said by some to be the best railway ever built. He also built two grand stations – Paddington (London) and Temple Meads (Bristol).
- As a shipbuilder, Brunel designed three record-breaking ships:
- ✳ The *Great Western* – Launched in 1837, steam-powered and the biggest ship in the world. Crossed the Atlantic in a record 15 days.
- ✳ The *Great Britain* – Launched in 1843, the world's first all-iron ship with a screw propeller instead of paddles.
- ✳ The *Great Eastern* – Launched in 1858, again steam-powered and a new 'world's largest ship' record breaker. It carried 4 000 passengers and laid the first underwater communications cable between America and Britain.
- In 2002, BBC TV asked people to vote for 'the Greatest Briton'. In the end, Winston Churchill came first … but Brunel came second. He got twice as many votes as Princess Diana!

▶ **Supporter No. 1:** Written by a university Professor, from 'Investigating History, 1750–1900', J D Clare

'Isambard Kingdom Brunel took engineering to the top … he gave everybody hope. People came to believe that humankind could do anything it wanted to do and go anywhere it wanted to go.'

▶ **Supporter No. 2:** The modern historian, Susan Willoughby, in 'Britain, 1750–1900'

'Britain needed engineers between 1750 and 1900. They designed roads, canals, locks, bridges, railways and tunnels. This was important work. It helped Britain to become a great industrial country. Brunel is a good example of an engineer at this time.'

'Man of steel'

- Born in 1813.

- A man of many inventions. He designed a machine for putting perforations on postage stamps, a way of making imitation velvet and a new method of producing glass.

- In 1856, he was also asked by the Government to make a cannon that wouldn't shatter under the force of a shell being fired from it. The army had been using iron cannon but felt that steel was better. It was stronger and less brittle for a start. But steel was very, very expensive to produce.

- Bessemer invented a 'converter', a machine for turning iron into steel (see **Source B**). Soon all the pots, pans, tools, furniture, ships, bridges, railways and machinery that had been made from iron were made from steel instead. Bessemer himself made 100% profit every other month for 14 years!

- In 1850, Britain produced 60 000 tons of steel – by 1880, over 2 000 000 tons were produced.

◀ **Source B** The huge container is filled with a white-hot liquid iron. A blast of hot air is blown through the bottom of the container. This removes many of the **impurities**. After a few chemicals are added to the swirling hot mass, the container is full of steel. Simple, eh!

'With Henry Bessemer's invention of his converter in 1856, steel could at last be made from iron quickly and cheaply. Steel was stronger and less brittle than iron and many new uses were found for it. Railways were re-laid with steel track. Great steel bridges were built to carry the lines over wide rivers… Steel also brought a great change to shipbuilding. It was lighter than iron, so bigger ships could be made.'

'Steel-making was a slow and expensive process and so Bessemer started work on a cheap, reliable way of making steel. In 1856, he came up with the idea of the converter… In about 20 minutes, the iron was pure and small amounts of carbon and manganese were added to it to make mild steel. This type of steel is neither as brittle nor as hard as cast steel [the more expensive type]. It is ideal for making girders, rails, tools or wire ropes.'

'The electricity king'

- Born in 1791, the son of a blacksmith.

- Worked in a bookshop where he became fascinated by science. He taught himself all he knew!

- He was most interested in electricity and magnetism and, in 1831, discovered how to generate electricity.

- His generator worked on the same basic principle that electric power stations work on today. The rim of a copper wheel passes between the poles of a magnet. When the wheel turns, electric current flows in the copper.

- When Faraday died in 1867, it was discovered that he had kept notes on EVERY aspect of his research – he always numbered the paragraphs of his notes, the last paragraph being number 3299.

'An example of a pure scientist was Michael Faraday, who devoted his life to the discovery and understanding of electricity… Faraday's experiments led to such inventions as the telegraph, the telephone and electric light … [and] … allowed him to claim to be regarded as the father of modern technology.'

▼ **Source C** Faraday at work in his laboratory

▶ **Entrant No. 5: George Stephenson**

'The father of the railways'

- Born in 1781.
- First job at 14 was working at the local coal mine with his father.
- Designed his first steam locomotive, the *Blucher*, in 1814 – but it was no quicker than using horses to pull coal wagons.
- In 1815, he produced a safety lamp for miners, which could be used safely in areas where methane gas had collected.
- In 1821, he was given the job of designing the Stockton to Darlington Railway. It opened in 1825 and used his company's locomotives.
- Designed and made locomotives for the first city-to-city line – Liverpool to Manchester – which opened in 1830.

▼ **Source D** An old £5 note – Stephenson's image was replaced in 2002

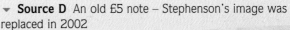

▶ **Supporter No. 2:** The Bank of England's old £20 note

The Bank of England thought Faraday was so important, they once put his image on a £20 note.

▶ **Supporter No. 1:** Written by modern historian, Bob Fowke, in 'Who? What? When? Victorians'

'Before the coming of the railways, the fastest anyone could travel was the speed of a galloping horse. By the time George Stephenson retired, you could travel from London to Newcastle by train in just nine hours, at an average speed of approximately 28mph. It was Stephenson, the son of a fireman in the Northumberland mines, more than anyone else, who created the British railway system ... before he retired in 1845, he had designed most of the railway which connects the major cities of the North of England.'

▶ **Supporter No. 2:** Written by modern historian, Bea Stimpson, in 'The World of Empire, Industry and Trade'

'The railway was a major gift that Britain gave the world. A newspaper article of 1864 claimed that no discovery since the invention of printing had exercised so great a change and produced such remarkable and beneficial results for the whole human race.'

▶ **Entrant No. 6: James Watt**

'Mr Power'

- Born in 1736, Watt was an instrument maker at Glasgow University.

- In 1764, Watt was asked to repair an old steam engine. These engines were used mainly in mines to pull out water, but were slow and kept breaking down. They only produced an 'up and down' motion.

- Watt greatly improved the older steam engine. He made it faster and more reliable. It used less coal too!

- In 1773, Watt and his partner, Matthew Boulton, designed a steam engine that could turn a wheel. This is called **rotary motion**. Now steam power could be used to drive machinery.

- By 1800, Watt and Boulton's factory in Birmingham was producing some of the finest steam engines in the world. Gradually, steam power replaced horse, water, wind and muscle power.

▶ **Supporter No. 1:** By modern historian, Bea Stimpson, in 'The World of Empire, Industry and Trade'

'… by 1800, there were nearly 500 Boulton and Watt steam engines in use. This machine, by replacing hand and muscle power in many industries, transformed the lives of hundreds and thousands of workers.'

▶ **Supporter No. 2:** Written by modern historian, Peter Moss, in 'History Alive 3, 1789–1914'

'Long before 1800, the steam engine was pumping water and lifting cages in coal mines, working bellows and great hammers in ironworks and turning machinery in factories of all kinds … such an engine was obviously going to be used in transport too … there were steam cranes, steam ploughs, steam road trucks and even attempts to make steam flying machines… British trains and British ships carried goods made in British factories all over the world – and all of these depended on the steam engine.'

(!) WISE UP WORDS

patent   entrepreneur   impurities
rotary motion

HUNGRY FOR MORE?

These six pages don't mention every great inventor or designer. Far from it! Many items that we take for granted today were dreamed up by these ten clever clogs between 1750 and 1900.

Try finding out a bit more about some or all of these people (there are a few non-Brits in there too).

Sir Humphry Davy – *miners' safety lamp*

Joseph Swan – *light bulb*

William Fox Talbot – *photography*

Thomas Edison – *lots of things!*

Alexander Graham Bell – *telephone*

Auguste and Louis Lumière – *moving pictures*

Guglielmo Marconi – *radio*

Wilhelm Röntgen – *X-rays*

Joseph and Jacques Montgolfier – *hot air balloon*

Leclanche Cell – *batteries*

▼ **Source E** One of Watt's steam engines, designed in 1788. This one is on display in the Science Museum, London.

WORK

1 Imagine you work for the organisers of the special award ceremony. You've been given the job of writing the programme that is given out to each guest as they arrive. Prepare the programme using this guideline:

- Plan the programme carefully – will you use A5 or A4 paper?
- Write clearly – writing drafts to begin is always best!
- Give facts, dates and figures about each inventor or designer. What did they invent or design? When? How?
- Only pack the programme with information; do not say how you feel about each one or why one is better than the other.
- Include a front cover, mentioning the name of the award ceremony and the six contenders.

2 Have a debate: 'Who deserves our National Award for Invention and Design, 1750–1900?'

a Choose a favourite inventor or designer: Arkwright, Brunel, Bessemer, Faraday, Stephenson or Watt.

b Write a persuasion text about your favourite, trying to get people to agree that he deserves the award. Use powerful adjectives that will make your favourite seem great, for example, '_____ was amazing because…'. Mention how important their contribution was to the field of invention and design between 1750 and 1900, for example, '_____ was important because…'.

c Six pupils could volunteer to speak, one for each of the inventors or designers. In turn, each speaker should try to persuade the class to vote for their man.

d After each speech, it's time to decide who deserves the award. Hold a class vote, perhaps in secret, to decide who wins.

How 'great' was the 'Great Exhibition'?

AIMS
▸ Why did the Great Exhibition take place?
▸ Was it a success, or not?

On 1 May 1851, Queen Victoria and her husband, Prince Albert, opened the Great Exhibition. It was held in London's Hyde Park in a huge, specially built hall, made of glass and metal. It was the world's first **international** exhibition and was designed to show the very latest and finest goods you could find anywhere in the world. Nothing like this had ever been done before and Queen Victoria was as excited as anyone – she visited twice even before the exhibition officially opened!

What could people see?

The exhibition was Prince Albert's idea. He wanted the world to see how fantastic Britain and her Empire was. In total, visitors could see over 100 000 exhibits from Britain, her colonies and 39 foreign countries. Visitors could walk through a French section, a Chinese gallery, or even an Indian room. There were separate areas for modern machines, arts and crafts, and manufactured goods. Items on display included: a full-size steam train; a printing press that printed 100 000 sheets of newspaper in one hour; a massive diamond called the Koh-i-noor and champagne made from rhubarb.

▾ **Source A** The Great Exhibition, designed in just ten days by Joseph Paxton, a gardener famous for building greenhouses.

- The building was 564 metres long and 140 metres at its widest point.

- 4572 tons of iron framework supported 293 655 panes of glass. The glass was transported by train from glassmakers in the Midlands.

- It took nine months to build and cost £335 742.

- It was the first large public building to contain free toilets for the visitors to use.

▲ Source B The Indian room was one of the most popular sections. It contained, among many other things, an enormous stuffed elephant!

How popular was it?

The exhibition attracted over six million visitors – about one third of all people in Britain! The new railways ran special trains from all over the country to London so that ordinary workers could see the exhibition. Visitors could not only walk around all day for 5p; they could buy a huge range of food and drink. A new company, Schweppes, provided many of the drinks on sale and a steam-powered freezer made ice cream on the spot!

The exhibition made a huge profit too – about £200 000. Prince Albert believed that the money should be used to encourage 'useful knowledge', so he spent it building the Victoria and Albert Museum, the Science Museum, the National History Museum and the Royal Albert Hall. All of these places are still going strong.

What did people say?

All sorts of protests were made against the building. Some said that a gust of wind could blow it all down and kill everyone inside. Others said that so many people would come into contact with each other that another great plague may hit Britain. One big worry was that the windows would get covered in bird droppings – and you couldn't shoot the birds in case you missed and smashed the windows. It was only when someone suggested using birds of prey to scare off other birds that a solution was found.

Most people loved the Great Exhibition. They didn't just enjoy the displays, but the actual building itself. Some called it a 'Palace of the People', whilst others just referred to it as the 'Crystal Palace'. Queen Victoria herself called it 'one of the wonders of the world'.

So where did the building go?

The Great Exhibition closed after six months. Britain had shown the world what a great nation she was and had enjoyed showing off. For the next 20 years, Britain dominated world trade as many countries became desperate to buy British goods.

The building itself was taken to pieces and moved to south-east London. A huge garden was built around it that attracted visitors for many years. A sports ground was built nearby which was used for FA Cup Finals until 1914 (and a football club was formed to use the pitch too … they called themselves Crystal Palace FC!).

Sadly, the building was destroyed by fire in 1936. Now only the gardens remain. Even Crystal Palace FC had to move to another ground!

 WISE UP WORD

international

HUNGRY FOR MORE? *Design an exhibition today that celebrates the country we live in. What would the exhibition be like? Write a proposal or make a presentation that includes a plan or description of the building and the kind of exhibits you would include.*

WORK

1 a Why was the Great Exhibition held?

   b What contributions did these people make to the exhibition?

   i) Joseph Paxton ii) Prince Albert

2 Imagine you are a Victorian visitor to the exhibition. Write a letter to a friend about your fantastic day.

   • What was the building like? Use facts and figures.

   • What did you see? Don't just write out a list; write what you felt about what you saw.

   • Use lots of powerful verbs and adjectives.

   • Why is the exhibition so popular? Write down reasons for its success – like everyone else, you have been amazed by what you have seen so try to persuade your friend that it was fantastic.

So what was the Industrial Revolution ... and why did it happen?

AIMS
▸ Who first used the label '**Industrial Revolution**'?
▸ What do historians think caused the Industrial Revolution?

Historians like to give labels to different periods of time – the 'Ice Age', the 'Stone Age', the 'Norman Conquest', the 'Middle Ages' and the 'Tudor Period' are all good examples. The period of time covered in this book, 1750 to 1900, also has a label. These two pages aim to discover how it got its name ... and what caused this Industrial Revolution to happen.

It was a British writer, Arnold Toynbee (1852–1883), who first used the label 'Industrial Revolution'. He was using it to describe the huge changes that had occurred in the way people worked in the years after 1750. This was the time when the **manufacturing** of all kinds of goods moved out of people's homes and into the new steam-powered factories. Dozens of clever, new machines made all sorts of goods in a fraction of the time it would have taken someone to make in their own home. By 1830, one operator working several factory machines could produce three-and-a-half thousand times more cloth than a person working at home could have done in 1700! It is easy to see why Toynbee used his label – 'industrial' is another word for 'work' and 'revolution' is an alternative word for 'change'. Certainly then, between 1750 and 1900, industry in Britain had undergone a massive revolution.

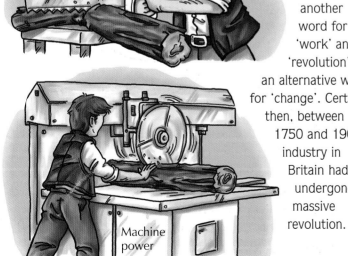

Muscle power

Machine power

As the years have passed, the label 'Industrial Revolution' has not just meant changes associated with the way people worked. It is now used to describe the changes that took place in the period of time as a whole – changes in the population, transport, towns and cities, medicine, science and technology and so on. Today, these changes are said to have happened 'during the Industrial Revolution'. So why did the Industrial Revolution take place?

Most historians agree that there weren't just one or two things that caused the Industrial Revolution to start. Instead, there was a combination of five or six factors that all came together in the same country at a similar time.

There were more people

Between 1750 and 1900, the population increased – massively. All these people needed shirts, trousers, coats, socks, shoes, plates, knives, forks, clocks and so on. The factories that produced these goods made a fortune for their owners – and there was plenty of work to go round too! Britain changed as factories were built to provide work for the growing population ... and made lots of goods for them to buy.

Britain gained an empire

During this time, Britain gained a huge empire. At one point, Britain ruled about 450 million people living in 56 colonies all over the world. Britain ruled huge countries

like Canada, India, Australia – and most of America – up to 1783. Britain's was the biggest empire the world had ever known! These colonies bought British-made goods of all kinds, especially cloth, iron and later steel. British traders were happy to sell as much as they could.

Britain changed as its empire grew. Cheap goods, like cotton, were imported from the colonies; the factories turned it into cloth ... and sold some of it back for huge profits!

There were some clever entrepreneurs

Entrepreneurs are business people who are prepared to take risks. They buy **raw materials** (like clay), make it into goods (like teapots) and sell the goods for a profit. Between 1750 and 1900, there were large numbers of risk-taking entrepreneurs. Banks were willing to lend them money to put into new businesses, factories and inventions if they looked like they would give them a profit.

There were many brilliant inventors

Between 1750 and 1900, some of the world's greatest inventors happened to live in Britain. Clever inventors thought up wonderful machines that produced more food, more cloth and more iron faster than ever before. Steam engines, steam trains, electric generators, telephones and light bulbs are just a few 'British Firsts'. Britain changed as it became a world leader in technology.

Britain had lots of coal and iron

Britain was blessed with some valuable raw materials. By 1850, Britain produced two-thirds of the world's coal, half of the world's iron, two-thirds of the world's steel and half of the world's cotton cloth! No wonder Britain was sometimes called the 'Workshop of the World'. Others just called it 'Great Britain'.

> **! WISE UP WORDS**
>
> Industrial Revolution   manufacture
> raw materials

WORK

1 In your own words, explain what the label 'Industrial Revolution' actually means.

2 All the following factors were important in creating an 'Industrial Revolution' in Britain. Your task is to show how these factors <u>worked together</u> to bring about the Industrial Revolution:

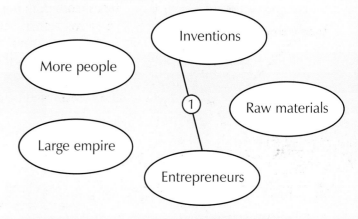

Key: ① Entrepreneurs were able to take the new inventions and make them into profitable businesses. This created jobs and wealth.

a Copy the diagram into your book.
b Then draw lines between those factors that you think are connected in some way.
c Give each line a number and below your diagram, explain the connection between the factors.

To help you get started, one connection has been drawn and explained.

Have you been learning?

Task 1

This wordsearch includes the names of ten people who have been mentioned in your studies so far.

Each time you find a name, log it down and write one sentence explaining why he was so famous.

A	A	R	K	W	R	I	G	H	T	N	O	K
K	M	L	O	A	G	E	N	T	L	E	R	F
I	J	S	A	T	B	O	O	G	C	C	E	W
P	L	K	I	T	H	D	A	R	B	Y	M	B
G	H	G	S	R	I	H	G	B	A	C	E	T
B	R	I	N	D	L	E	Y	E	S	F	S	E
L	E	V	I	O	J	U	H	G	S	V	S	L
B	R	I	D	G	E	W	A	T	E	R	E	F
E	M	N	F	B	I	R	C	H	A	A	B	O
O	S	T	E	P	H	E	N	S	O	N	M	R
N	N	B	P	C	D	S	U	T	E	A	C	D
Y	T	B	A	C	A	B	R	U	N	E	L	I
G	F	A	R	A	D	A	Y	H	Y	U	T	Y

Task 2

The two paragraphs below don't make much sense. They need capital letters, commas, apostrophes and full stops.

a Copy the paragraphs, adding punctuation as you write.

between 1750 and 1900 the population of britain grew very fast in 1750 there were about seven million people living in britain with another three million living in ireland however by 1900 britains population shot up to nearly 40 million

the places where people lived had changed too in 1750 only two out of ten people lived in towns whilst the rest lived in the countryside by 1900 many people had left the countryside and moved into the towns a census of 1901 showed that over 70% of people were now living in towns

b Answer the following questions:
  i) Give at least five reasons why the population grew so rapidly between 1750 and 1900. Explain your reasons carefully. You might want to refresh your memory by looking at pages 8 and 9.
  ii) Why did people move from the countryside to the towns?

Task 3

Of all the different characters and people you have learned about so far, who is most likely to have said each of the following statements? Write a paragraph to explain the choices you have made.

a 'The smaller children are very useful. They can crawl under the machines to tidy up and pick up bits of cotton.'

b 'I spend my days pushing and pulling loaded wagons from the coalface to the lift.'

c 'They are a nightmare – full of deep holes filled with water and mud. A simple ten-mile journey can take a whole day. And there's always the threat of robbery by highwaymen…'.

d 'I hate it here. I work long hours for little pay and get beaten when I make the smallest mistake. There's always the risk of losing a finger on the unprotected machinery too!'

e 'I've been asked to build a 20-mile rail track from the port of Stockton on Tees to a coal mine in Darlington. I want to use steam locomotives on the track.'

f 'It is a wonderful exhibition. I've seen a huge diamond, a seat made from coal, a full-size steam train and a metal-making machine. I've even tasted champagne made from rhubarb.'

Task 4

As you have learned, many factories had very strict rules. Workers were fined if they didn't obey them. Play the 'Rules Game' with your friends and see who escapes with the smallest amount of fines!

You will need:

- 2, 3 or 4 players
- six pieces of paper, numbered 1 to 6, or a die
- a blank copy each of the **Record of Fines** sheet (see below – why not copy one out?)

RECORD OF FINES		
DAY	**OFFENCE**	**FINE**
MONDAY		
TUESDAY		
WEDNESDAY		
THURSDAY		
FRIDAY		
SATURDAY		
	TOTAL FINES	

How to play:

- The game begins on Monday. Player 1 picks a number (which should be folded up so no one can identify it!) or throws the die.
- Look at the **Game Chart** and read along Monday until you match your number to a letter. For example, if Player 1 throws a 2, their letter would be 'D'.
- Look up your offence on the **Factory Rules** notice. These are real rules and fines from a factory near Leeds in 1844.
- Fill in your fine on your **Record of Fines**.
- All other players choose numbers and fill in their **Record of Fines** for Monday.
- Move onto Tuesday.

The winner:

When all fines are added together, the winner is the one with the least amount of fines.

GAME CHART						
	Number thrown					
Day of week	**1**	**2**	**3**	**4**	**5**	**6**
MONDAY	C	D	A 10 mins	F	A 5 mins	☺
TUESDAY	A 15 mins	☺	B	E	B	C
WEDNESDAY	F	F	C	A 5 mins	B	D
THURSDAY	D	☺	☺	B	C	F
FRIDAY	B	C	A 10 mins	D	E	F
SATURDAY	☺	C	D	☺	☺	A 5 mins

FACTORY RULES

A Late for work: 5 minutes = 2p fine; 10 minutes = 5p fine; 15 minutes = 10p fine

B Leaving room without permission = 3p fine

C Whistling, singing or talking = 2p fine

D Swearing or failing to follow instructions immediately = 5p fine

E Leaving the workplace in an untidy way = 2p fine

F Feeling ill and failing to find someone to do your job for you = 4p fine

☺ A good day = no fine!

4 • Terrible towns

A question of class

AIMS
- How divided was British society?
- What did a typical middle-class house look like?

Benjamin Disraeli, a famous Victorian writer and politician, once wrote that Britain was made up of two nations – a rich nation and a poor one. What do you think he meant? Was he right? You've studied how the poor lived their lives … so what about those with a bit more money?

Historians use the word 'class' to describe a particular group of people, based mainly on the amount of money they earn, their houses and their social life. In Victorian Britain, there were three main classes. Firstly, poorer people like those we have studied in this book so far, the ones who worked long hours in the factories and the mills and lived in the cramped, disease-ridden housing, were known as the **working class**. This class made up 70% of the population. Secondly, there was the **middle class**. This group included the factory owners, mine owners, businessmen, doctors, lawyers and other professionals. Some of these people were very rich indeed and had the lifestyle to go with it. These people made up approximately 25% of the population. Finally, there was the **upper class** – the mega-rich, royalty, dukes, duchesses, lords and earls.

The overcrowded centres of towns were clogged with shops, factories and busy dirty streets. This is where the poor people lived – the labourers and the factory hands, the shop assistants and the servants. Just outside the centre were larger, better built terraced houses (some with small gardens), occupied by highly-paid workmen, such as mechanics, engineers, factory **clerks** and skilled craftsmen. On the edges of towns would be the houses of the more wealthy – doctors, lawyers and bank managers for example. These 'posher' areas on the edges of towns were known as the **suburbs**.

▼ How the different classes in a typical town might be divided. Why do you think the richer people built their homes in the areas where the wind didn't blow towards them?

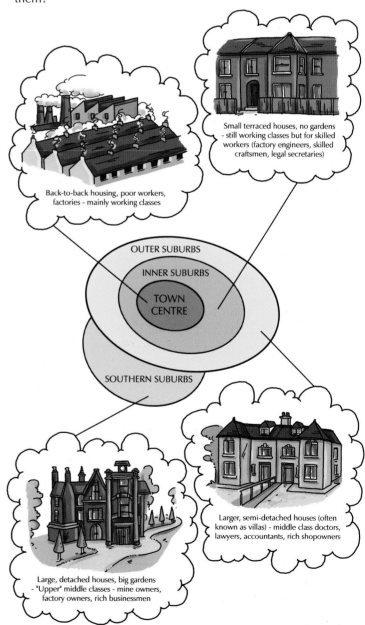

Small terraced houses, no gardens - still working classes but for skilled workers (factory engineers, skilled craftsmen, legal secretaries)

Back-to-back housing, poor workers, factories - mainly working classes

OUTER SUBURBS
INNER SUBURBS
TOWN CENTRE
SOUTHERN SUBURBS

Larger, semi-detached houses (often known as villas) - middle class doctors, lawyers, accountants, rich shopowners

Large, detached houses, big gardens - "Upper" middle classes - mine owners, factory owners, rich businessmen

 WISE UP WORDS

clerks   suburbs   middle class
working class   upper class

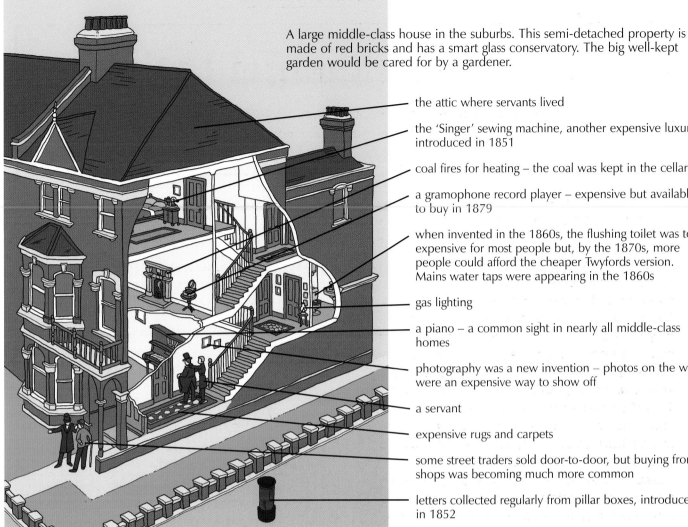

A large middle-class house in the suburbs. This semi-detached property is made of red bricks and has a smart glass conservatory. The big well-kept garden would be cared for by a gardener.

the attic where servants lived

the 'Singer' sewing machine, another expensive luxury, introduced in 1851

coal fires for heating – the coal was kept in the cellar

a gramophone record player – expensive but available to buy in 1879

when invented in the 1860s, the flushing toilet was too expensive for most people but, by the 1870s, more people could afford the cheaper Twyfords version. Mains water taps were appearing in the 1860s

gas lighting

a piano – a common sight in nearly all middle-class homes

photography was a new invention – photos on the wall were an expensive way to show off

a servant

expensive rugs and carpets

some street traders sold door-to-door, but buying from shops was becoming much more common

letters collected regularly from pillar boxes, introduced in 1852

FACT: ▶ Monday's meals

▶ In 1899, Seebohm Rowntree (his family made chocolate) interviewed two families in York. He asked them what they ate on Monday. No prizes for guessing which family was rich and which was poor.

Family 1

Breakfast: Porridge, fried bacon, toast, butter, treacle, marmalade, tea and coffee

Dinner: Boiled mutton (sheep), carrots, turnips, potatoes, bread sauce, jam roly-poly pudding and rice pudding

Tea: Bread, teacakes, butter, cake and tea

Supper: Fish, bread, butter, cake, biscuits, cocoa and oranges

Family 2

Breakfast: Bacon, bread and tea

Dinner: Bacon, bread and tea

Tea: Bacon, bread and tea

Supper: Nothing

WORK

1   Write a sentence or two to explain the following:
    suburbs • working class • middle class • upper class

2   a   Copy and label the town plan from page 50 into your book.

    b   Why do you think the poorer, working-class people lived near the centres of towns?

    c   Why do you think the richer people lived in the suburbs or out in the countryside?

3   Look at the meals for the two families:

    a   Which family do you think was poor and which was rich? Give reasons for your answers.

    b   Why do you think the members of the rich family would have lived, on average, for approximately 20 years longer than the poor family?

4   Look at the diagram of the middle-class house. What basic differences are there between this house and the place where you live?

What made Sheffield stink?

▶ Why did towns grow in the nineteenth century?
▶ What was it like to live in some of these places?

In 1850, the writer Charles Reade visited the town of Sheffield. He didn't stay long! When he got home, he described Sheffield as 'perhaps the most hideous town in creation'. He reported that black smoke blocked out the sun. He wrote that 'sparkling streams entered the town ... but soon got filthy, full of rubbish, clogged with dirt and bubbling with rotten, foul smelling gases'. So what made Sheffield stink? And why was Sheffield – and many other towns like it – turning into such a disgusting place to live?

Sheffield was no different to many other English towns at this time. Towns like Manchester, Leeds, Liverpool, Birmingham, Nottingham and Bolton were equally as bad. Yet each of these towns had existed for hundreds of years. Why then, did they become such horrible places to live?

The answer lies in one simple fact: once a factory was built, perhaps making cloth, iron or pottery, people would flood in from the countryside in order to find work.

▼ **Source A** In 1801, only eight towns in England, Wales and Scotland had more than 50 000 people living there: Birmingham, Bristol, Edinburgh, Glasgow, Leeds, Liverpool, London and Manchester. By 1900, there were over 60.

Town	Population 1750	Population 1801	Population 1851
Liverpool	35 000	82 000	376 000
Birmingham	30 000	71 000	233 000
Leeds	14 000	53 000	172 000
Manchester	45 000	75 000	450 000
Sheffield	12 000	45 000	150 000

▼ **Source B** A Government report of 1842

'Broken panes in every window frame, and filth and vermin in every nook. With the walls ... black with the smoke of foul chimneys, without water ... and sacks for bed clothing, with floors unwashed from year to year.'

▼ **Source C**
Top diagram: A plan of **back-to-back** housing
Bottom diagram: A cross section of a typical street

L = Lavatory   P = Pump   = Heaps of human manure

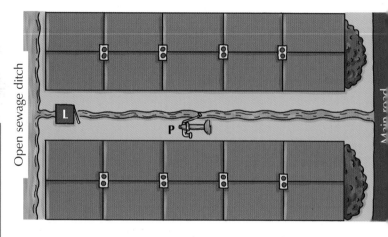

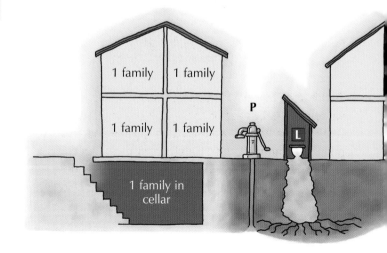

▲ **Source D** Dirty Sheffield

▼ **Source E** Edwin Chadwick, 1843

'I spent my holiday visiting the worst towns with Mr Smith, Dr Playfair and Sir Henry de la Beche. Dr Playfair has been seriously ill and Mr Smith has had terrible diarrhoea. In Bristol, Sir Henry stood up at the end of an alley and vomited while Dr Playfair was investigating overflowing toilets.'

▼ **Source F** From a newspaper report of 1845

'In one group of 26 streets … the ground was covered with sewage which leaked into the cellars. A pool, over a metre deep, and filled with this stinking fluid, was found in one cellar under the bed where the family slept.'

The factory owners then had to build homes for the workers, usually nearby so that people could walk to work. These houses were built as quickly and cheaply as possible, crammed close together with narrow streets between them. Built in rows or **terraces**, the houses were built back-to-back to save space and money.

Almost all the houses were crowded, five or more people living in one small room. In 1847, 40 people were found sharing one room in Liverpool!

None of these houses had toilets either. The best some families could manage was a bucket in the corner of the room, which would be emptied now and again, either into the street or stored outside the door until there was enough to sell to a farmer as manure. Occasionally, there was a shared street toilet (a deep hole with a wooden shed over it) but this would be shared by 30 or 40 families. Sometimes a water pump provided water, but often the water only came from the local river or pond and this would be as filthy as the water in the streets.

Sewage trickled down the streets and constantly flowed into nearby rivers. Yet most families washed their clothes, washed their bodies and drank from the same river. It was little wonder that terrible diseases were common. There were no rubbish collections, street cleaners, sewers and no fresh running water. And nobody seemed to care!

No wonder Sheffield stank!

WISE UP WORDS

terraces   back-to-back

WORK

1 a Draw the plan of back-to-back houses in your book.
   b What is missing from these houses that we take for granted today?
   c On your plan, mark which house (or houses) you would *least* like to live in. Give reasons for your choice.
   d How might these living conditions lead to poor health and disease?

2 a Look at **Source A**. Draw a bar chart to represent the growth in population of each of the five towns. Your teacher will help you plan this out.
   b Why did these towns grow so quickly?

3 Look at **Source E**.
   a What made Sir Henry vomit?
   b Do you think Sheffield, and other places like it, were healthy places to live? Give reasons for your answer and use some of the sources to back up your opinions.

Welcome to Sickness Street

AIM ▶ What were the most common diseases in the nineteenth century?

Disease thrived in towns. In 1840, one in every five children died before their first birthday and one in three died before they reached five! In Manchester, the average age of death for an ordinary working man was 17! Astonishing! People had been attracted to towns by the promise of jobs in factories. But the reality of living in the **squalor** of these ever expanding towns was the particularly bad effects on people's health. So what did people die of in these places?

▲ A photograph of back-to-back houses in Staithes, Yorkshire

FACT: ▶ Typhoid

▶ **How?** Germ lived in urine and poo! Sometimes this **contaminated** water or food. Urgh! This killer disease could also be carried by flies, which land on food.

▶ **Symptoms?** Headaches, fever, **constipation** … then terrible diarrhoea. A similar disease called **typhus** was common too, caused by bites from body lice.

▶ **Who?** Can attack anyone.

FACT: ▶ Tuberculosis

▶ **How?** Germs are passed from one person to another in the moisture sprayed when people cough or sneeze. Sometimes called 'consumption'. Another type of TB was caused by infected cows' milk. Why do you think this infected more children than adults?

▶ **Symptoms?** Attacked the lungs. A victim would cough up blood, lose weight, get a fever, chest pains and shortness of breath. Can kill.

▶ **Who?** Can attack anyone. Infected one out of ten people in the nineteenth century.

FACT: ▶ Smallpox

▶ **How?** Germs are passed from one person to another by coughing, sneezing, or in some cases touching.

▶ **Symptoms?** A rash turns into huge pus filled blisters all over the body. When the blisters drop off, they leave deep scars. Can kill.

▶ **Who?** Can attack and kill people of all ages.

FACT: ▶ Cholera

▶ **How?** Caused by a germ that lived in contaminated water. It was the end for any human who drank the water.

▶ **Symptoms?** 'Cholera' is the Greek word for diarrhoea. As the diarrhoea became worse, the victim could keep no food or water in his or her body. They would **dehydrate** and die – sometimes within 24 hours.

▶ **Who?** Can attack anyone. In Britain, 32 000 people died from cholera in 1831, 62 000 in 1848, 20 000 in 1854 and 14 000 in 1866. These were known as **epidemics**.

In filthy overcrowded places like Leeds and Manchester, diseases spread very quickly. The average age of death in Leeds was 19! But, unlike today, ordinary people in the towns didn't know that germs could cause disease. Far away in laboratories, some doctors had started to make the connection, but down in the streets and slums of Britain, people continued to live their lives and get their filthy water in the same way that they had always done. It would be many years before the health problems caused by the rapid growth of the towns were tackled.

WISE UP WORDS

squalor   contaminated   constipation
typhoid   typhus   tuberculosis   smallpox
cholera   dehydrate   epidemic

▼ **Source A** Based on official records of some people who died of cholera in Merthyr Tydfil, Wales, in 1866.

FACT: ▶ Prince Albert

▶ Were the rich as likely to die as the poor? In December 1861, Prince Albert, husband of Queen Victoria, caught typhoid and died. He was 42. The filthy water from one of his palace toilets had leaked into his drinking water.

▼ **Source B** A doctor describes a street in Scotland, for a Government report of 1842

'There is a huge dunghill here. The owner sells it. He gets more money for older dung! The pile smells so badly that people nearby have to keep their food covered because it tastes of the dunghill!'

No	When taken ill (all 1866)	When died	Where died	Sex	Age	Occupation	Habits	Contact with infection?	State of neighbourhood
1	23 August	25 August	31 Quarry Row	M	32	Fireman	Good and clean	No	A drain, which carries away house slops, runs under house.
2	23 August	26 August	13 Morris Court	F	75	Rag cleaner	Clean	Might have picked up dirty rags	Gully at end of court is steeped with excrement. House has no ventilation.
3	24 August	25 August	7 Canal Street	M	21	Factory worker	Regular	No	Open sewer behind house, covers floor, offensive.
4	24 August	1 September	16 Sunny Bank	F	53	Wife of a tailor	Dirty	No	Cesspool in garden overflowing. Floor of sleeping room covered with excrement.
5	25 August	27 August	1 Miles Court	M	8	Son of a labourer	Dirty	Had travelled about neighbourhood	Cesspool near house full and overflowing.
6	28 August	1 September	9 Sunny Bank	F	40	Wife of a miner	Clean	May have visited No. 4	Overflowing cesspool.

WORK

1 Write a sentence or two to explain the following words:
squalor • contaminated • epidemic

2 Using the facts on page 54, copy these headings in your book and complete the information:
Name of killer disease
How did people catch it?
What happened when they got it?
Why was it so common? **TOP TIP**: Think how living conditions made it more likely to catch.

3 Read **Source A**.
a Write down at least two things that all the cholera victims had in common.

b How do you think victim No. 6 caught cholera?

4 Read **Source B**.
a What did the owner of the Dunghill do with his dung?
b Who might have wanted to buy his dung – and why?
c How did the dunghill affect people in the neighbourhood?

5 a How did Prince Albert die?
b Does his death surprise you? Give a reason for your answer.

Crimewatch, 1800

 AIMS
▶ What are **capital crimes**?
▶ How were crimes punished during the early 1800s?

A life of crime was a very easy one in 1800. Many criminals were never caught because there were no policemen to track them down. Some places had **constables** to keep an eye on things, but these men weren't very effective. They were unpaid and were only chosen to do the job for a year before someone else took over. Many were careful not to do the job properly – they didn't want to be chosen again! Other towns had **watchmen** to keep law and order. Watchmen were paid (very badly though) and were seen as a bit of a national joke. They were often so old, or feeble, or too drunk to catch anyone that, in some areas, crime had become the number one problem.

If, by some slim chance, a criminal was caught, the law showed little mercy. Many people felt that criminals should be savagely punished so as to act as a warning to others. Indeed, in 1800, there were over 200 crimes for which a guilty person could be executed!

Some Capital Crimes
(Crimes for which you could be hanged)

Theft of anything worth 5 shillings (25p) or more

Murder, treason or piracy

Cutting down growing trees

Damaging Westminster Bridge

Kidnapping

Coining

Stealing a sheep

Pretending to be a pensioner of Chelsea Hospital

Plus about 180 other crimes

An amazing statistic, one which is difficult to believe today, is that one out of every eight prisoners found guilty of a crime in 1800 were sentenced to death … and the public loved to go and watch the executions. In fact, a public hanging was a day out for all the family and huge crowds turned up to watch. In 1802, 28 people were killed in a crush at a hanging outside Newgate Prison in London. Some richer people paid to rent out houses overlooking the **gallows**, and seats in specially built grandstands fetched high prices.

▼ **Source A** Adapted from 'Travels in England', by Thomas Platter, 1799

"The guilty men are placed on a cart, each with a rope around his neck. The cart was driven off under the gallows. Then the criminals' friends come and pull them down by the feet so that they might die all the sooner."

Yet despite the popularity of these public hangings, fewer people were hanged than should have been. Courts often took pity on young children or desperate men and women and found them not guilty … even if they had clearly committed a capital crime!

PAUSE FOR THOUGHT

In 1793, Michael Ascot was charged with stealing 43 pairs of socks worth £3 10 shillings (£3.50). Why do you think the jury found him guilty of only stealing socks to the value of 4 shillings 10d (24p)?

 WISE UP WORDS

watchman   constable   piracy   coining
gallows   transportation   pardoned
'pleads her belly'   capital crimes

Another common punishment in 1800 was **transportation** for either five, seven or fourteen years. This meant a terrible voyage in a prison ship to a British colony, such as Australia or Gibraltar. Once there, the prisoner would become a slave, working for one of the settlers, or perhaps used as a worker constructing roads or buildings. After the convict had served their sentence, they were free to return to England. Many never did (they couldn't afford the trip home) so settled for a new life abroad.

Study these fascinating criminal cases carefully. These are real people. Their crimes and punishments have been taken from official court records.

Name: Sophie Girton

Age: 25

Crime: 'She is charged with coining … that she, with Thomas Parker (aged 42), did make fake coins, mainly shillings and sixpences … and did then attempt to use them … this is an offence against the king.'

Verdict: Guilty (both of them)

Punishment: 'She is to be drawn on a hurdle to the place of execution and Sophie Girton is to be burnt.'

Notes: Her accomplice, Thomas Parker, was hanged. According to court records, it seems that Sophie Girton was possibly the last woman to be burned at the stake in England!

Name: Elizabeth Anderson

Age: 13

Crime: 'She did steal one leather bag and three silk sheets from a cloth shop … the goods were valued at ten pennies.'

Verdict: Guilty

Punishment: Whipped in the pillory and then held in Newgate Prison for one year.

Notes: It didn't matter how young you were! Criminal kids often ended up in England's filthy jails or even on prison transport ships. In 1790, ten-year-old Joe Davis was transported to Australia for stealing a pair of trousers. Punishments could be a lot worse than that too! In 1792, a seven-year-old girl was hanged for stealing a dress. In 1802, a 12-year-old was hanged for stealing a sheep. In 1831, a nine-year-old boy was hanged for setting fire to a house.

Name: Hannah Ramsey

Age: 23

Crime: 'It is charged that she did steal a purse and a pistol valued at £2 and 5 shillings (£2.25).'

Verdict: Guilty

Punishment: Death by hanging … 'but Ramsey **pleads her belly**'.

Notes: Women who claimed they were pregnant at the time were sentenced to death could 'plead their belly'. These women (and there were lots of them) were examined by a group of women (chosen from spectators at court) and if found to be 'quick with child' (if movement of a baby was detected) their punishment was postponed until after the baby was born. Often the women were later **pardoned** because the court didn't want to have to deal with the problem of looking after an orphaned child. Hannah Ramsey was successful in her attempt to 'plead her belly'. Instead, she and her child were transported to Australia for seven years!

WORK

1 Why were most i) constables and ii) watchmen so unreliable? Explain each answer carefully.

2 a Explain what is meant by the phrase 'capital crime'.

  b Why were so many people sentenced to death in 1800?

  c Why were fewer people executed than there should have been?

3 Look at **Source A**.

  a Explain what happened at an execution.

  b Why do you think some of the friends of the guilty men pulled down on their feet whilst they were hanging?

4 Study the criminal cases carefully and answer the questions in full sentences.

  a What was Sophie Girton's crime?

  b Who do you think received the worst punishment – Sophie or her accomplice? Give reasons for your answer.

  c Why wasn't Hannah Ramsey hanged? Explain your answer carefully.

  d Was she punished at all?

  e Why do you think young Elizabeth Anderson wasn't hanged?

Who caught the vile Victorian villains?

AIMS
- How did the modern police force start?
- Why are policemen sometimes called 'bobbies'?

In 1750, it wasn't safe to go out at night in any large town or city. Thieves and robbers lurked in dark alleys and drunken brawls were heard all night long. Conmen, beggars and prostitutes pestered people constantly and pickpockets stole from any unsuspecting citizen. The crime rate was getting worse and criminals seemed to be getting away with more and more. So how could crime be stopped? Who could make the streets safer?

An MP called Sir Robert Peel thought that he had an answer to the crime problem. As part of his job as **Home Secretary**, he was responsible for dealing with law and order. So in 1829, he set up Britain's first official police force. It was known as the Metropolitan Police Force and at first, just dealt with the city with the biggest crime problem – London.

Three thousand men were **recruited** to begin with (women were not allowed to join). They had to be less than 35 years of age, healthy and able to read and write. They were given new blue uniforms (with silver buttons), boots, a wooden **truncheon**, a rattle,

▼ **Source A** One idea for avoiding stranglers. How do you think this funny outfit would stop an attacker?

handcuffs, a brown coat and a top hat lined with iron. They received 5p a day (not much in 1829, but better than a lot of other jobs) and were expected to walk their 'beat' seven days a week.

A policeman, 1829

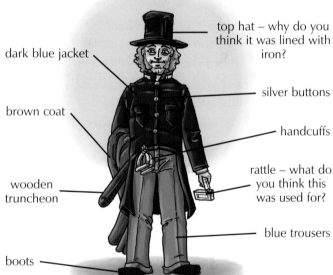

- dark blue jacket
- brown coat
- wooden truncheon
- boots
- top hat – why do you think it was lined with iron?
- silver buttons
- handcuffs
- rattle – what do you think this was used for?
- blue trousers

To begin with, people hated the new police force. Some felt that they were a threat to an Englishman's freedom and policemen were regularly beaten up in the street and spat at. Early nicknames included 'Peel's bloody gang' and the 'evil blue devils'. But these 'blue devils' did a very good job. They were well disciplined, good-humoured and acted with **restraint** whenever possible. Gradually, the public began to respect and trust them. More criminals were caught so there was less crime in London too. Soon other towns copied the example set by London's police and, by 1856, every town in the country had its own policemen. In 1829, there were 3 000 policemen and 18 000 convictions for major crimes. By 1900, there were about 48 000 policemen and 25 000 convictions. A new police force had been born and it seemed to be working.

▼ **Source B** Instructions given to policemen in 1829

'You must be polite and attentive to everyone. Rudeness will not be tolerated. You must act quickly and sensibly and have a perfect temper, never allowing yourself to be moved by any foul language or threats … police constables are asked not to pay any attention to any silly expressions which they may be called.'

 PAUSE **FOR** **THOUGHT**

Early policemen were called 'Peelers'. No prizes for guessing how they got this nickname! But they were also known as 'Bobbies' (they still are). Why do you think that the first policemen got this nickname?

▼ **Source C** 'Bobbies on the beat'. A very early photograph of some of Britain's first 'boys in blue'.

WORK

1 a Explain why Sir Robert Peel set up Britain's first official police force.

   b Why were some people against the police at first?

2 a Copy the picture of the 1829 policeman. Label your picture clearly.

   b Why do you think he:
      i)   carried a truncheon?
      ii) carried a rattle?
      iii) wore a top hat lined with iron?

3 Imagine you are looking for a job in 1829 and you see an advertisement asking for new policemen. Using your knowledge of the type of person Peel was looking for, write a letter of application for one of the vacancies:
   • Why do you want the job?
   • What qualities do you possess?
   • Why should Peel pick you?

 WISE UP WORDS

Home Secretary   recruited   truncheon   restraint

Meet Charles Sheppard, prisoner No. 43

AIMS
- ▶ What was it like in a nineteenth-century prison?
- ▶ Why was prison life so tough?
- ▶ How did prisons change?

Meet 14-year-old Charles Sheppard. He's in Shepton-Mallet Jail awaiting trial on a charge of 'stealing a parcel containing five or six knives'. He is cold, dirty and starting to feel ill – and he hasn't been found guilty of anything yet! One thing's for sure though – you wouldn't want to be a prisoner in 1805.

Charles: 'Life is tough. We are forced to work on pointless tasks all day long. We pace the treadmill, a sort of large wheel that goes nowhere; we call it 'the everlasting staircase'. Sometimes we unpick old ropes and turn them into doormats, but I hate this most of all because my fingers bleed!'

▼ **Source A** A tale of an escaped prisoner in 1800

'On his arrival at the Fleet Prison, he was stripped naked and thrown into a dark dungeon just above the prison sewer. Occasionally, food was thrown down to him and a fellow prisoner, feeling sorry for him, found him an old mattress. On Sunday, Arne escaped and ran towards the chapel while Sunday service was being held. The feathers from the mattress were sticking into his naked body, making him look like a "repulsive bird". He was taken back to his cell and locked up again.'

Charles: 'The cells are filthy and we haven't got enough light, water or proper food. We get bread and porridge every day, but it's never enough. The water we get is so dirty it makes us feel sick to taste it. We don't get provided with beds either but can hire them from the jailors at six pence per night. I can't afford one, so I sleep on the floor on two old rugs that were left over when another prisoner died. I share my bed with the rats, lice and fleas.'

In 1805, conditions inside prisons were dreadful – so bad, in fact, that visitors sometimes wore nose clips or handkerchiefs soaked in vinegar so they couldn't smell the prisoners. There was no clean water supply or sewage system and disease was so common that it killed about 25% of the prisoners each year.

▶ **Source B** 'The everlasting staircase'

Charles again: 'The jailors who run this place don't get paid - they make their money by selling us food, beer, tobacco and blankets. Those who can afford it eat and drink well. The rest of us live on local charity. We get charged for everything in here. There are fees for admission, fees for release, fees for food, fees to have your leg irons removed for a few hours a day - it's endless. Even if you're found innocent, if you can't pay any of the money you owe, you stay inside. Madness!'

A man called John Howard was so shocked by the conditions in the prisons near his home that he wrote a best-selling book about them, called The State of Prisons. One woman went further than that. After being appalled by what she saw on a visit to Newgate Prison in 1813, Elizabeth Fry spent the rest of her life trying to clean up the country's prisons and help the prisoners. She even went into prisons to read Bible stories to the inmates, taught them to read and write and even helped them to tidy up their cells.

Soon the Government began to take notice of Elizabeth Fry and John Howard. Prisons began to change. They still remained a tough, uncomfortable place to be, but conditions inside them improved. By 1900, official Government figures showed that the milder treatment led to fewer men returning to prison after their sentence.

PRISON REFORMS

Jailors paid wages (so prisoners were not charged for everything!)

Women prisoners kept separate from the men

Prison doctors and teachers appointed

Prisoners to be taught to read and write

Prison inspectors appointed

FACT: A more civilised country?

▸ With the new police force catching the criminals and the prisons being less tough, Parliament was persuaded to make punishments less harsh. After 1841, the only crimes for which hanging remained were murder, treason, violent piracy (being a pirate) and burning down a dockyard or an arsenal (where weapons are stored). In 1868, public executions were stopped and transportation was ended. The country seemed to be getting more civilised!

PAUSE FOR THOUGHT

You will see a picture of Elizabeth Fry at least every week – but where? Clue: it makes the world go round.

WORK

1. a Why did some visitors wear nose clips or cover their faces with handkerchiefs soaked in vinegar?
   b Why was disease so common among prisoners?
   c Why did jailors charge prisoners for the things they wanted?

2. a How did these people contribute to the improvement of prison life?
      i) John Howard
      ii) Elizabeth Fry
   b How had prisons improved by 1900? Give examples to support your answer.

3. Charles Sheppard spent 13 weeks in jail waiting for his trial. When the time came, his accuser failed to turn up at the courthouse – and Charles walked free. Choose any three days in Charles' 13-week stay in jail. Write a diary entry for each of the three days.

4. What do you think is meant by the sentence, 'The country seemed to be getting more civilised'? Explain your answer carefully. You may want to discuss it as a class first.

HISTORY MYSTERY

What did 'Jack the Ripper' look like?

On 31 August 1888, a London **prostitute** called Mary Ann Nichols was found murdered. Her throat had been slashed with a long-bladed knife and her stomach had been cut open. Then, just over a week later, another prostitute called 'Dark Annie' Chapman was found dead in a backyard only a few hundred metres from the first murder. Her throat had been cut, her body torn open and some of her internal organs had been placed over her shoulder. Some other body parts had disappeared too!

The police realised they had a serial killer on their hands. They needed to track him (or her) down quickly … before they struck again!

▾ **Source A** A photo of the backyard of 29 Hanbury Street, the place where the body of 'Dark Annie' Chapman was found.

A few weeks after the second murder, a London newspaper received an amazing letter (see **Source B**). The writer boasted of the killings and teased the police for not catching him.

Within weeks, the name 'Jack the Ripper' would become famous all over Britain – and the 'Jack the Ripper' legend would be born!

▾ **Source B** Adapted from 'Jack's' letter, 27 September 1888

Dear Boss,

I keep on hearing the police have caught me but they haven't. I have laughed when they look so clever and talk about being on the right track. I am down on whores and I shan't quit until I get caught. The last job was good work. I gave the lady no time to squeal. How can they catch me now? I love my work and want to start again. You'll soon hear of me. I saved some of the red stuff in a ginger beer bottle so I could write to you with it, but it went thick like glue and I can't use it. Red ink is fit enough I hope, ha, ha. The next job I shall cut the lady's ears off and send them to the police for fun. My knife's so sharp I want to get to work right away if I get a chance. Good luck.

Yours truly,
Jack the Ripper
Don't mind me giving the nickname
PS They say I'm a doctor now, ha, ha!

PAUSE FOR THOUGHT

Why do you think the police thought 'Jack' was a doctor or a butcher?

In 'Jack's' letter (**Source B**), what do you think the 'red stuff' was that he was writing about?

What was 'Jack' intending to do with the 'red stuff'?

On 30 September, two more prostitutes were murdered. 'Long Liz' Stride and Catherine 'Kate' Eddows were killed and cut up within minutes of each other. Police found graffiti near the body of Catherine Eddows saying 'The Jews did it', but they washed it off. Bits of her blood-soaked clothing were nearby. Later, doctors found that one of her ears, her nose and some of her kidney had been removed!

◄ **Source C** A **mortuary** photograph of Elizabeth Stride, murdered on the same night as Catherine Eddows

▼ **Source D** The gravestone of Catherine Eddows

CITY OF LONDON CEMETERY

Here lie the remains of
CATHERINE EDDOWS
Age 43 years
Buried 8 October 1888
Victim of 'Jack the Ripper'

On the morning of 1 October, the newspaper received another letter (see **Source E**). The letter makes reference to the 'double-killing' the night before. Many experts still believe these first two letters are from the real killer.

▼ **Source E** The second letter

I wasn't kidding dear old Boss when I gave you the tip. You'll hear about Saucy Jacky's work tomorrow. Double event this time. Number one squealed a bit – couldn't finish straight off. Ha, not the time to get the ears off for police.

Jack the Ripper

On 16 October, the police received another letter. The envelope contained a note and a piece of human kidney! However, the police were unable to tell if the letter came from the same person as the first two letters or if the kidney came from Catherine Eddows.

▼ **Source F** Letter sent to police, 16 October 1888

Sir,

I send half the kidney I took from one of the women. I cooked and ate the other half. It was very nice. I might send you the knife.

Catch me if you can

On 9 November, a fifth prostitute was murdered. Mary Kelly's body was found inside her own rented room. She was the only 'Ripper' victim to be found indoors. She had been cut open, her organs had been placed around the room and her face had been hacked beyond recognition. Now five women had been killed within a mile of each other in a poor area of London called Whitechapel. Some policemen thought that other murders could be linked to the 'Ripper' – as many as 13 – but the detective in charge of the case, Fred Abberline, decided to keep the figure at five.

Source G A map of the Whitechapel area of London showing where each victim was found.

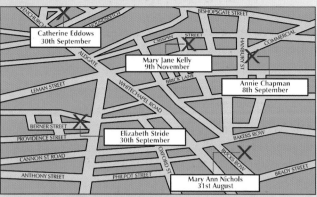

By mid-November, news of the 'Jack the Ripper' killings had spread all over the world. Stories appeared in 160 newspapers in countries as far away as Mexico and Australia. The police were under pressure to catch the killer and even Queen Victoria said the killer must be caught quickly.

The police interviewed over 2 000 people, including witnesses who had claimed to have seen some of the victims with 'mysterious looking' men shortly before their deaths. Police talked to sailors, butchers, doctors, writers and drug addicts. They even handed out over 80 000 leaflets asking for information.

However, the crimes were committed in an age before forensic science and fingerprinting. The only way to catch the killer was to see them commit a crime or get them to own up.

For the police, their hopes rested with their key witnesses who claimed to have been near one murder scene on the night of the killing. Had they seen the 'Ripper'?

Source H This is a summary of each of the witness statements. The source gives the witnesses' name, the murder scene they were near, the time they sighted the 'Ripper' and a description of him. Read each report carefully – you are trying to work out what 'Jack the Ripper' looked like.

Ripper files

Name of witness	Near to which scene was the Ripper seen?	Time of sighting	What did the Ripper look like?
Emily Walter	Annie Chapman	2:00am	Foreigner aged 37, dark beard and moustache. Wearing short dark jacket, dark vest and trousers, black scarf and black felt hat.
Elizabeth Long	Annie Chapman	5:30am	Dark complexion, brown deerstalker hat, possibly a dark overcoat. Aged over 40, somewhat taller than Chapman. A foreigner.
J Best and John Gardner	Elizabeth Stride	11:00pm	5'5" tall, English, black moustache, blond eyelashes, weak, wearing a suit and a hat.
William Marchall	Elizabeth Stride	11:45pm	Small, black coat, dark trousers, middle aged, round cap with a small sailor-like peak. 5'6", stout, appearance of a clerk. No moustache, no gloves, with a coat.
Matthew Packer	Elizabeth Stride	12:00–12:30pm	Aged 25–30, clean-shaven and respectable appearance, 5'7", hard, dark, felt deerstalker hat, dark clothes. Carrying a newspaper parcel 18 x 7 inches.
James Brown	Elizabeth Stride	12:45am	5'7", stout, long black coat which reached almost to his heels.
Israel Schwartz	Elizabeth Stride	12:45am	**First man**: Aged 30, 5'5", brown haired, fair complexion, small brown moustache, full face, broad shoulders, dark jacket and trousers, black cap with peak.
			Second man: Aged 35, 5'11", fresh complexion, light brown hair, dark overcoat, old, black, hard felt hat with a wide brim, clay pipe.
Joseph Lawende	Catherine Eddows	1:30am	Aged 30, 5'7", fair complexion, brown moustache, coat, red neckerchief, grey peaked cloth cap. Sailor-like.
James Blenkinsop	Catherine Eddows	1:30am	Well-dressed.
Mary Ann Cox	Mary Kelly	11:45pm	Short, stout man, shabbily-dressed. Hat, blotchy face, carroty moustache, holding can of beer.
George Hutchinson	Mary Kelly	2:00am	Aged 34–35, 5'6", pale complexion, dark hair, slight moustache curled at each end, long dark coat, dark jacket underneath. Light waistcoat, thick gold chain with a red stone seal, dark trousers and button boots, gaiters, white buttons. White shirt; black tie fastened with a horseshoe pin. Dark hat turned down in middle. Red handkerchief. Jewish and respectable in appearance.

Amazingly 'Jack the Ripper' was never caught. The killings just suddenly stopped. The police identified many suspects but never charged anyone with the crimes (see **Source I**). To this day, the killer's identity remains a mystery, yet his crimes have inspired at least 12 movies, four TV series and over 200 books. Many experts, or **Ripperologists** as they are known, are no closer to solving the crimes than they were in 1888 ... perhaps we will never know the truth!

▼ **Source I** Main 'Ripper' suspects – over the years, many writers and historians have claimed to know who the real 'Ripper' was ... but no one has ever proved anything. Here are some of the main suspects. Is 'Jack' amongst them?

Dr Thomas Cream

An American doctor who had been arrested for poisoning prostitutes and writing false letters to the police. He was hanged in 1892 for murdering prostitutes. His last words were 'I am Jack'. However, he was in prison at the time of the last three 'Ripper' murders.

Severin Klosowski (AKA George Chapman)

Suspected by police at the time of the murders. Had poisoned two of his wives. Trained as a doctor, worked as a barber near Whitechapel.

M J Druitt

A lawyer and teacher. Trained as a doctor. His own family thought he could be the 'Ripper'. Committed suicide in December 1888. There were no more murders after this time.

Alexander Pedachenko

Possibly called Michael Ostrogg too. A Russian doctor who worked in a women's hospital. Went back to Russia shortly after the last murder and was sent to a mental hospital for the murder of a woman in St Petersburg.

Prince Albert Victor (Grandson of Queen Victoria)

Was known to hang around the gay bars in Whitechapel. A keen hunter. Suffered from a brain disease and secretly married a woman his family disapproved of. Mary Kelly, the last victim, worked for him for a short while. Did she know his secrets? Did she tell the other murdered prostitutes? Did he kill them to keep them silent?

HUNGRY FOR MORE?

There were other 'Ripper' suspects – an artist named Walter Sickert, a cotton merchant named James Maybrick and an American doctor named Francis Tumblety. Some people even thought it might be Lewis Carroll, the writer of Alice in Wonderland.

- *Why not try to find out more about the main suspects?*
- *Prepare a factfile on each suspect (research on the Internet or in the school library).*
- *Perhaps hold a class discussion or trial for each suspect.*
- *Write an essay entitled 'Who was Jack the Ripper?'*

! WISE UP WORDS

prostitute   whore   Ripperologist   mortuary

WORK

Using the witness statements, design a 'WANTED' poster for 'Jack the Ripper'.

- Draw a full length 'artist's impression'.
- Include a BEWARE file warning the public what to watch out for: physical appearance, usual clothing, approximate age, 'killing time', favourite 'haunts' and any other useful information.

TOP TIP: Make sure you do a draft copy, then a neat one on A3 paper – it will make a great class display.

5 • Britain's Empire

An Empire to be proud of?

 AIMS

▸ What was the British Empire?
▸ Why did Britain want an **empire**?

Between 1750 and 1900, the British conquered many foreign lands. Approximately 13 million square miles of territory was ruled by Britain by 1900 – this was about one quarter of the world! This was some achievement – but is it one to be proud of today?

Study this painting carefully (**Source A**). The **Maori** tribesmen are signing over their land to the British. They are exchanging their whole country – New Zealand – for guns and alcohol!

▾ **Source A** This event took place in 1840. Before the British arrived, the Maoris had no idea that people could own land – they believed it belonged to everyone.

British settlers soon divided up their land and fenced it off. It is highly unlikely that the tribesmen would have agreed to any deal if they fully understood what it meant. In later years, when some Maoris objected to the way they were treated, the British showed them no mercy. Thousands were killed. Successive wars against the British in New Zealand reduced their population from about 100 000 to 35 000 by 1900. This is just one example of the methods by which Britain increased her empire in the period 1750 to 1900.

So how did Britain gain an empire?

British explorers and settlers would travel to different regions of the world and claim the land for Britain. To the British, it didn't matter that people already lived there – the British generally had better weapons so the **natives** had to accept their new rules. The British did this time and time again, all over the world – in Africa, Australia, India and New Zealand for example.

These new lands were known as **colonies** and an empire was a collection of colonies all ruled by one country. The British Empire then was a muddle of different regions, islands and countries spread all over the world. The empire grew steadily between 1750 and 1900.

So why did Britain want an empire?

There were two main reasons for the creation of the British Empire: one involves money and the other involves God.

Money, money, money...

Colonies offered cheap **natural resources**. When the British took over South Africa for example, they gained some of the world's best diamond mines. They got sugar from the West Indies, cotton from Egypt and tea from India. Other resources obtained from the colonies included meat, wool, silk, spices, gold, rice, chocolate, rubber and palm oil. The more places Britain controlled, the more natural resources they could lay claim to.

Colonies also offered excellent outlets for trade in the many manufactured goods Britain's industries were pouring out. Traders brought back goods from colonies to sell on at high prices in Britain and also raw materials that would be processed and turned into products in Britain's factories. Then, finished goods could be exported back to the colonies and the rest of the world. At every stage of the process, someone was making money from trade.

By taxing the profits made by British traders, the British Government made millions of pounds. Part of this money was used to improve Britain's army and navy, providing them with the best weapons and latest ships. This further helped to reinforce Britain's control over her colonies.

▼ **Source B** Imports and exports 1700–1900 (£millions)

Year	Imports (goods brought to Britain)	Exports (goods sold to other countries)
1700–1709	4.8	6.1
1740–1749	7.3	9.9
1800–1809	28.7	37.6
1840–1849	79.4	141.5
1900–1909	570.4	333.3

God Almighty

One passage of the Bible says, 'Go ye therefore and teach all nations' (Matthew 28:19). Some British Christians took this to mean it was their duty to bring Christianity to the 'godless' people of the newly discovered lands. Christians who travelled abroad to try to convert people to Christianity were called **missionaries**. These people would try to convert the chief of a tribe first, hoping the rest of the tribe would follow.

> ! **WISE UP WORDS**
>
> superior   natural resources   Maori   missionaries
> uncivilised   empire   natives   colonies

▼ **Source C** A nursery rhyme from a baby book, printed in 1899

> C is for colonies
> Rightly we boast
> That of all the great nations
> Great Britain has the most

In other places like India, the British didn't try too hard to convert the different religions (200 million Hindus, 60 million Muslims, six million Sikhs and two million Buddhists). Instead, they introduced the British way of life and language. They felt that their way of life was **superior** to the **uncivilised** Indians.

▼ **Source D** James Morris, 'Pax Britannica', 1968. Quoted in Ros' Adams 'Expansion, Trade and Industry' (1992). The area he is writing about was Ceylon (now called Sri Lanka).

> 'Over the next 80 years, the British built 2 300 miles of road and 2 900 miles of railway. They raised the area of land for farming from 400 000 acres to 3.2 million acres, the livestock from 230 000 to 1.5 million, the post offices from 4 to 250, the telegraph lines from 0 to 1 600 miles, the schools from 170 to 2 900, the hospitals from 0 to 65, the annual amount of goods shipped abroad from 75 000 tons to 7 million.'

WORK

1   Look at **Source A**.
   a   Write a sentence or two to explain the word 'Maori'.
   b   Explain how the British took advantage of people who didn't fully understand them.
   c   What happened to the Maori population of New Zealand between 1840 and 1900?

2   List and explain the reasons why Britain wanted an empire.

3   a   What was a 'missionary'?
   b   Suppose you are a missionary in one part of the British Empire. Write a letter home explaining what you hope to do and how your mission will help the native people.

4   a   According to **Source D**, what advantages did British rule bring to Ceylon?
   b   Does this mean that British rule was a good thing then? Explain your answer carefully.

By 1900, Britain ruled about 450 million people living in 56 colonies all over the world. The British Empire was the largest empire the world had ever known and the British people were very proud of their acquisitions. Most people didn't believe for one second that the empire might be wrong; they thought that their empire was good for Britain … and good for the world. What do you think?

Canada – in 1750, Canada was a French colony and the British had their eyes on it. They thought it might have the new 'cash crops' of tobacco and sugar. In 1759, General James Wolfe led a British army to Canada and beat the French. Many British people then **emigrated** there (despite the ten-week voyage) for a new life. By 1865, three million people lived there, making money from cattle and wheat farming. In 1867, Britain granted Canada more freedom to run its own affairs.

India – In the 1700s, the British East India Company traded with Indian princes for silk, tea, spices and other valuable goods. It used its private army to get land for Britain. In 1857, the Indians **rebelled** against the British. The Indian Mutiny, as the rebellion became known, was crushed in a very brutal fashion by the British. After 1859, the British Government started to run India directly. A **viceroy**, appointed from Britain, was put in charge of the country and Queen Victoria gave herself an extra title – Empress of India. The Victorians thought India was Britain's number one colony at this time – 'the jewel in the crown' as they called it. In fact, the massive Indian Koh-i-noor diamond was taken and added to the British Royal Crown.

West Indies – Britain seized many of these islands from the Spanish and Portuguese between 1650 and 1800. Many black Africans were taken there to work as slaves for the British colonists. Even today, the official language of Trinidad, Tobago, Barbados, Jamaica, the Bahamas and other islands is English.

THE INDIA & COLONIAL EXHIBITION,
LONDON, 1886.
MAP OF THE WORLD
SHEWING THE EXTENT OF THE
BRITISH EMPIRE IN 1886.
British Territories Coloured Solid Blue, and also as this GIBRALTAR

Africa – British slave traders had been taking black Africans to America and the West Indies since Tudor times. Between 1880 and 1900, there was a 'scramble for Africa' as European countries divided up most of the continent. Britain took over control of 16 colonies. In South Africa, the British encountered fierce resistance to their takeover, first from native Zulu warriors and then from Dutch and French settlers, known as Boers. Between 1899 and 1902, Britain lost over 20 000 men in the Boer Wars trying to take complete control of South Africa.

Australia and New Zealand – Captain Cook reached Australia in 1770 and claimed it as a British colony. Yet thousands of natives, known as **Aboriginals** already lived there! From 1788, the British used Australia as a prison and transported thousands of convicts to the colony. When many convicts finished their sentences, they stayed in Australia and farmed the land. Gold was discovered in the 1850s and many people went to Australia to search for it. By 1900, about four million people lived in Australia. New Zealand had become a British colony in 1840 (see **Source A**).

A Victorian map of the British Empire from 1886. The colonies are shown in blue. Some of the people (and animals) who lived in the Empire are pictured around the map.

▼ **Source E** A leaflet written by Indians who wanted the British out. Who do you think the thieves were?

'Can these thieves really be our rulers? These thieves … import a huge number of goods made in their own country and sell them in our markets, stealing our wealth and taking life from our people. Can those who steal the harvest of our fields and doom us to hunger, fever and plague, really be our rulers? Can foreigners really be our rulers?'

▼ **Source F** The British settlers took land from the Aboriginals. They were often hunted and killed for sport! In 1802, the British arrived in Tasmania (the island south of Australia). The island contained 20 000 native Aboriginals. Eighty years later, there were NONE!

? DID YOU KNOW?

- America was a British colony for many years. In 1750, Britain owned various large areas in what is now known as the USA. But people in these areas didn't see why they should continue to pay taxes, year after year, to a British Government they didn't even elect. In 1775, fighting broke out between the Americans and the British (who had sent an army over). On 4 July 1776, the Americans declared their **independence** from Britain (Independence Day is still celebrated every year in America). The War of Independence continued for another five years but the British eventually lost this valuable colony.
- America got its first president, George Washington, in 1789.

HUNGRY FOR MORE?

- *What is Britain's Empire like today?*
- *What places around the world can the British Government still call colonies?*
- *When did Britain 'lose' other colonies? Why?*

! WISE UP WORDS

emigrated   viceroy   Aboriginals
independence   rebel

WORK

1   Match the *Heads* in the first column to the *Tails* in the second.

Heads	Tails
Africa	Seized from the French in 1759. Many British people emigrated there soon after.
Australia	Became part of the British Empire in 1840.
Canada	Was seen by many as Britain's number one colony. Often known as the 'jewel in the crown'.
India	The British managed to take control of 16 areas of this huge continent between 1880 and 1900.
New Zealand	Many black Africans were transported to this group of islands to work as slaves for British settlers.
West Indies	Captain Cook reached this island in 1770. The British started using it as a prison from 1788.

2   Look at **Source E**.
a   Is this source in favour of British rule or against it?
b   Explain how you made your decision, perhaps using a quote or two from the source.

3   Look at **Source F**.
a   Who were the 'Aboriginals'?
b   How were they treated under British rule?

4   Why do you think many British sports, like rugby, cricket and football, are popular in countries that were once part of the Empire?

5   Write two paragraphs about the British Empire – one on something (or things) to be proud of, the other on something (or things) to be ashamed of.

Pg 109

The Great Hunger

AIMS

▶ What caused the 'Great Hunger'?
▶ Did the British Government do enough to help?

In 1997, the British Prime Minister, Tony Blair, made an apology on behalf of the Government. He said they were sorry for something that happened in Ireland in 1845. Mr Blair said that one million Irish people died as a result of something the English did. But what was he talking about? Was his statement correct? Do you think modern politicians should apologise for the actions of those long ago?

▼ **Source A** Tony Blair speaking in 1997

'One million people died, in what was, at that time, the richest country in the world. This still causes pain today. The English stood by and let a potato disease turn into a human disaster.'

In 1840, over eight million people lived in Ireland. Over half were poor peasants who rented tiny farms from landowners. Many of these landowners were English, from families who had taken the land from the Irish many years ago. Now the Irish had to rent land that had once belonged to them. This made them angry. Most of these peasants lived on nothing but the potatoes they grew in their fields. They couldn't even afford bread.

Since 1801, Britain had ruled Ireland from London. The British Parliament made all the decisions relating to Ireland, yet British laws meant that Catholics couldn't vote. As most of the poor Irish peasants were Catholics, this also made them angry.

In September 1845, a potato disease called **blight** started to destroy the potato crop. Millions were left without their main source of food. The same thing happened in 1846, 1847 and 1848. By the end of 1848, nearly a million people had died of starvation. Another million left Ireland altogether for a new life in America. By 1871, one quarter of New York's population was Irish!

▼ **Source B** From an eyewitness' account at the time of the **famine**, quoted in 'The World of Empire, Industry and Trade'

'Families, when all was eaten and had no hope left, took their last look at the sun, built up their cottage doors so that none might see them die nor hear the groans, and were found weeks afterwards, skeletons on their own hearths.'

▼ **Source C** Estimated population of Ireland in millions, 1760–1860

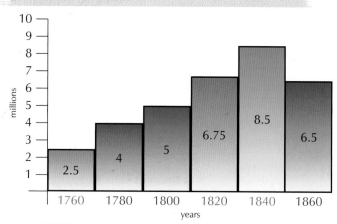

▼ **Source D** From an Irish newspaper, November 1846

'When the Queen [Victoria] at her coronation swore to protect and defend her subjects, no exception was made with regard to Ireland. How does it happen then that while there is a shilling in the Treasury or even a jewel in the crown that subjects are allowed to perish with hunger?'

▼ **Source E** Written by the modern historian, Andrew Langley, in 'Victorian Britain'

'The British Government was slow to give help. Worse still, it gave no protection to peasant farmers who were too poor to pay rents on their land. Many were evicted [thrown out] from their homes by the landowners, most of whom lived in England.'

▼ **Source F** A family waiting to be evicted from their home during the Great Hunger

▾ **Source G** Written by the modern historian, Duncan Gunn, in 'The Little Book of British History'

'One of the greatest natural disasters to strike the Western World in modern times, the potato famine that hit Ireland … resulted in more than one million deaths and the forced migration of a million more. Its effects would not have been a tenth as bad if the British Government of the time had made the slightest effort to relieve the starvation, and if … landlords had not made matters worse by evicting thousands of tenants from the land.'

▾ **Source J** Wheat imports and exports to Ireland 1844–1848 (in '000 tons)

Year	Exports (wheat sent *out* of Ireland)	Imports (wheat sent *into* Ireland)
1844	424	30
1845	513	28
1846	284	197
1847	146	889
1848	314	439

▾ **Source H** Written by the modern writer, Bea Stimpson, in 'The World of Empire, Industry and Trade'

'He [the British Prime Minister, Robert Peel] had ordered Indian corn and meal to be bought and handed out to the starving Irish. He initiated [started] public work schemes so that poor labourers could earn money … assistance in Ireland was limited to public works programmes [but] the schemes couldn't cope with the numbers, so were abandoned in favour of indoor relief, soup kitchens and workhouses … many were helped by voluntary workers. The Quakers [a Christian group] set up soup kitchens, the Guinness brewing family provided food and work, the British Relief Association gave funds and the New York Irish Relief Fund sent nearly £250 000.'

▾ **Source K** Adapted from a speech made by Mr Andrews, speaking in the Irish Parliament in 1995, quoted in 'Investigating History'

'I have read a lot about this in the summer, and I think it is wrong when people say we should forgive the English for something that happened 150 years ago. I cannot forgive them. They were to blame.'

▾ **Source L** Adapted from a speech by Mr Connor, talking in the Irish Parliament in 1995, quoted in 'Investigating History'

'I do not think the English Government tried to kill the Irish. There were famines in England at this time and the Government ignored them too, and left the people to die. This is what they were like in those days. They thought it was not the Government's job to feed people.'

▾ **Source I** Written by a British Government official in 1847. The man was actually in charge of the Famine Relief Association.

'It is my opinion that too much has been done for the Irish people. Under such treatment the people have grown worse instead of better … it is not the job of Government to give people food.'

◄ **Source M** This statue remembering the famine was erected in 1998 in Boston, USA. It was paid for by the Irish descendants of those who emigrated in the 1840s. In some parts of the USA, schoolteachers were instructed to teach pupils that the actions of the British Government in Ireland in the 1840s were similar to the actions of the Nazis against the Jews during the 1930s and 1940s.

 WISE UP WORDS

blight   famine

PAUSE FOR THOUGHT

Do you think it affects people's opinion of the famine if they are English or Irish? If so, say why.

WORK

1 a How did many Irish people feel about the British, even before the famine? Explain your answer carefully.

   b Why was the potato so important to many Irish people?

2 a What do **Sources B**, **D** and **E** tell you about how Irish people suffered during the famine?

   b How did some people escape from the famine?

3 Look at **Source G**.

   a According to this source, did the British Government make any effort to help the Irish people at all?

   b Do you think this is true? You may wish to look at **Sources H** and **J** before answering.

4 According to **Source L**, why did the British Government do so little to help people?

5 Look at **Source M**.

   a Why do you think so many Americans are interested in the famine?

   b Do *you* think the British Government's actions during the famine were as bad as Hitler's attempts to kill all the Jews?

6 Hold a class debate. Your debate should focus on two areas:

   i) Did the British *try* to kill the Irish people?

   ii) Was Tony Blair right to apologise for the famine?

   Your teacher will help you to organise and structure your preparation and discussions.

What was the slave trade?

AIMS

▶ How did the slave trade start?
▶ To what extent were the British involved?
▶ How did the slave trade operate?

The idea of slavery is a very old one. For thousands of years, men have captured 'weaker' people and forced them to do their work. The Egyptians used slaves to build the pyramids and the Romans forced them to fight in gladiator arenas.

From about 1500 onwards, some men started to turn slavery into a profitable business. **Slave traders**, many of them British, made a fortune by taking young men, women and children from their homes in Africa, sailing them across the Atlantic Ocean and forcing them to work on the huge cotton, sugar and tobacco farms of North America, South America and the West Indies.

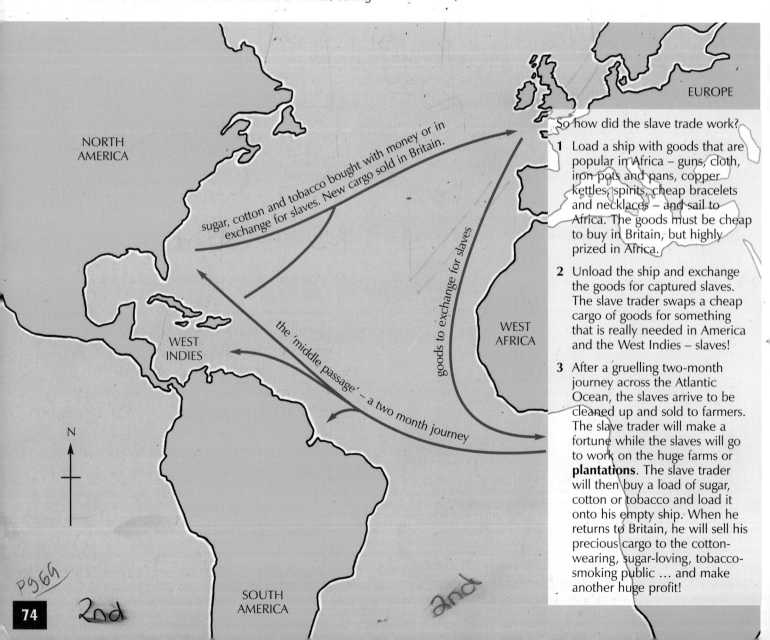

NORTH AMERICA

EUROPE

sugar, cotton and tobacco bought with money or in exchange for slaves. New cargo sold in Britain.

goods to exchange for slaves

WEST INDIES

WEST AFRICA

the 'middle passage' – a two month journey

N

SOUTH AMERICA

So how did the slave trade work?

1 Load a ship with goods that are popular in Africa – guns, cloth, iron pots and pans, copper kettles, spirits, cheap bracelets and necklaces – and sail to Africa. The goods must be cheap to buy in Britain, but highly prized in Africa.

2 Unload the ship and exchange the goods for captured slaves. The slave trader swaps a cheap cargo of goods for something that is really needed in America and the West Indies – slaves!

3 After a gruelling two-month journey across the Atlantic Ocean, the slaves arrive to be cleaned up and sold to farmers. The slave trader will make a fortune while the slaves will go to work on the huge farms or **plantations**. The slave trader will then buy a load of sugar, cotton or tobacco and load it onto his empty ship. When he returns to Britain, he will sell his precious cargo to the cotton-wearing, sugar-loving, tobacco-smoking public ... and make another huge profit!

▲ **Source A** Slave traders at work: a painting of slave dealers on the coast of Africa

▶ **Source B** This was the official coat of arms for an English slave dealer. He designed it himself and had these crests carved into most of his furniture in his London home!

▼ **Source C** This account was written by a slave who was taken to work in the West Indies. Years later, he was freed and taken to England.

'I saw many of my miserable countrymen chained together, some with their hands tied behind their backs. We were taken to a place near the coast and I asked the guide why we were here. He told me that I was to learn the ways of the white-faced people. He took a gun, some cloth and some metal in exchange for me. This made me cry bitterly. I was then taken to a ship where I saw my fellow captives moaning and crying.'

 WISE UP WORDS

slave trader   plantation

WORK

1 Write a sentence or two to explain the following words:

   slave trader • plantation

2 a In your own words, explain how the slave trade was organised. Use a diagram to help you.
   b Why was the slave trade so profitable?
   c The slave trade is often referred to as 'triangular trade' or 'the slave triangle'. How do you think it got its name?

3 Look at **Sources A** and **C**. What similarities can you find between the scene in the painting and **Source C**?

4 Look at **Source B**.
   a Draw the coat of arms, writing a description next to your picture.
   b Why do you think the English slave dealer decided to use this image as his official coat of arms?

On board the *Brookes*

AIMS

▶ How did the slaves end up on board a slave ship?
▶ What were conditions like on board?
▶ How were the slaves treated?

African men, women and children were usually captured by warriors from other tribes. Some were sent to be traded because they had broken the laws of their own tribe by committing crimes. They were taken to holding camps and kept in cages until a slave trader and his ship arrived. They were then exchanged for goods and loaded onto the ships. One slave, Ottobah Cogoano, was one of the very few slaves to survive his journey on board ship and write his story down years later. He told how he was exchanged for a gun, a piece of cloth and some metal!

The slave ship Brookes was just one such ship. Based in Liverpool, it made several journeys to Africa, America and then back to Britain. We know about it because its owners kept detailed records about its journeys. After all, the slave trade made big money so traders treated their job like any other professional business.

The Brookes could carry over 400 slaves, crammed together into tiny spaces below deck. The distance between the main slave decks was only 1.5 metres, so the slaves couldn't stand up or turn around and the chains and shackles bit into their legs (see **Source B**). Men were loaded in the bow (the front), boys in the centre and women in the stern (back part of the ship).

▼ **Source A** This eighteenth-century illustration shows slaves being loaded on board ship for an Atlantic crossing.

▼ **Source B** A plan of the Brookes. No space was wasted.

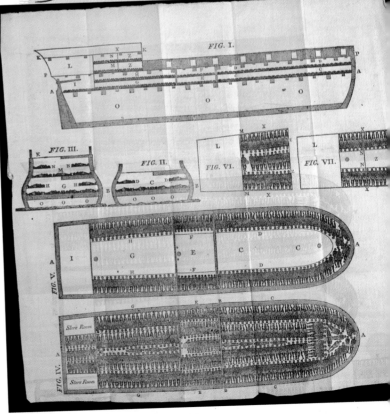

▼ **Source C** Taken from the 'Journal of a slave trader', 1788. Written by an ex-slave trader, John Newton.

'The poor creatures, thus cramped for want of room, are likewise in irons, for the most part both hands and feet, and two together, which makes it difficult for them to turn or move, to rise or lie down, without hurting themselves.'

Living conditions were horrific. Temperatures below deck could reach 35°C and seasickness and heatstroke were very common. So too was **dysentery**, a nasty form of diarrhoea. The only toilet was a bucket but many couldn't reach it so they ended up lying in their own waste … and everyone else's.

Olaudah Equiano, another slave who survived to tell his story, said that children, unsteady on their feet due to hunger and the sea, often fell into the toilet tub and almost suffocated.

▼ **Source D** Written by a doctor after a visit to a slave ship

'The floor was covered with blood and mucus. It looked like a slaughterhouse. After 15 minutes down there I had to leave. The heat and the stink made me nearly faint.'

▼ **Source E** From Bea Stimpson's 'Black Peoples of the Americas'

'Some died of dysentery, "the bloody flux". Others died of harsh treatment and poor food. Some with infectious diseases, such as smallpox, were thrown to the sharks. Others went mad and were clubbed to death. Some committed suicide by hanging themselves or jumping ship.'

The journey lasted between 40 and 70 days and approximately ten million slaves were taken across the Atlantic in this way between 1510 and 1833. It is estimated that some two million died on ships like the Brookes during this time.

It may be hard for you to believe, but slave traders actually wanted the slaves to be in good condition when they arrived at their destination. So as they neared their destination, they were taken out to the top deck twice a day for exercise and given buckets of food to share out between groups of ten.

For those who survived the journey, the ordeal was far from over. They now faced the prospect of being cleaned up and sold!

WISE UP WORD

dysentery

WORK

1 a Why were so many slaves packed on board the ships?

   b Why do you think the slaves were chained together for most of the voyage?

   c Why do you think slave traders wanted slaves to be healthy and in good condition when they arrived? Does their treatment surprise you then?

2 a Copy and complete the following table:

Source	What does it show?	Why is it useful to us today?

   b Which source do you think is most useful to a historian? Give reasons for your explanation.

3 Many slave traders were very proud of the way they ran their businesses. They often invited observers on voyages to see the 'slave triangle' for themselves.

   Imagine you are one such observer, invited on the *Brookes* by a slave trader. Write a short letter to a friend, describing your journey and your feelings about the voyage.

4 a Each slave on the *Brookes* made an average of £22 profit when sold. If the ship carried 410 slaves, how much profit would the slave trader make in total?

   b Does profit make the slave trade a good thing? Explain your answer carefully.

A slave sale

AIMS
- How were slaves prepared for sale?
- How exactly were they sold?

Before any sale could take place, slaves were cleaned up. They were washed down with water and given oil or fat to rub into their skins. This made them look shiny and healthier. Hot tar or rust was rubbed into any sores or ulcers to disguise them. One ship's captain, whose slaves were suffering from terrible diarrhoea, instructed the doctor to push a thick piece of rope up the backside of each of them to block it for a while. Nobody would buy a sick slave so hopefully, the captain thought, this would be enough to fool his customers into a sale.

There were two main ways to buy a slave: **auction** or **scramble**.

'**Auction**' – slaves were paraded in front of buyers and examined like cattle. They were then made to stand on an auction box and buyers would 'bid' for them. They were sold to the person who paid the most. Unhealthy, unsold slaves were left to die without food or water.

'**Scramble**' – the slave trader would set a fixed price for his slaves. At a given signal, usually a horn or a drumbeat, the buyers would rush into the cage and grab the slaves they liked the best. You can probably tell why it was called a scramble!

▼ **Source A** A description by Olaudah Equiano, who was sold at a 'scramble'

'On a given signal, the buyers rush at once into the yard where the slaves are kept and make a choice of the one that they like best. The noise and clamour increases the worry of the terrified Africans. In this manner, relations and friends are separated, never to see each other again.'

▲ **Source B** A slave auction

FACT: ▶ Selling slaves

▶ In Jamaica in 1787, a slave called Jimmy fetched £330. He was a good carpenter 'in his prime'. At the same auction, a slave called Butler only fetched 6d (about 2.5 pence). He was described as 'a very **indifferent** fellow with bad legs'.

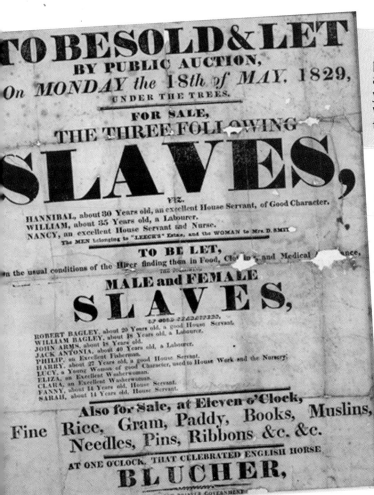

◀ **Source C** A poster advertising a slave sale. Can you see what else was being sold that day?

▶ **Source E** This is a branding tool. The new owner of a slave would burn his initials onto the slave using this.

! **WISE UP WORDS**

auction   scramble   indifferent   branded

WORK

1 a How and why were slaves cleaned up before they were sold?

   b What was a 'scramble'?

2 Look at **Source C**.

   a How many slaves were up for sale?

   b Describe how a slave auction works.

   c What do you think 'to be let' meant?

   d How many slaves were 'to be let'?

   e What would the hirer of a 'let' slave be expected to provide for them?

   f Which of the slaves up for sale would you expect to fetch the highest price? Give reasons for your choice.

   g Write a short paragraph explaining how a young person might feel if they were one of the slaves about to be sold or hired. Start your paragraph, 'I am going to the auction today. I feel…' .

   TOP TIP: You might want to brainstorm some of the words and emotions a slave might have felt as they approached the auction room.

3 Look at **Source D**. In your own words, explain why the woman in the story says that 'slavery is terrible'.

4 Look at **Source E**.

   a What was the purpose of this branding tool?

   b Why do you think the slaves were not allowed to speak their own language and were given a new name?

▼ **Source D** Written by Harriet Jacobs in her book, 'Life of a Slave Girl', in 1861

'I saw a mother lead seven children to the auction block. She knew that some of them would be taken from her; but they took all. The children were sold to a slave trader, and the mother was bought by a man in her town. Before night, her children were all far away. She begged the trader to tell her where he intended to take them; this he refused to do. How could he when he knew he would sell them, one by one, wherever he could command the highest price? I met the mother in the street and her wild, haggard face was today in my mind. She wrung her hands in anguish and exclaimed, "Gone, all gone! Why don't God kill me? Slavery is terrible."'

Once bought, slaves became the personal property of their owner. They were even given European names in an attempt to make them forget their past. Then, like cattle, they were **branded** with their owner's initials on their face, chest or back. They were now ready to start work.

A life of slavery

AIMS

▸ What sort of lives did slaves lead?
▸ Did any slaves rebel?

The slaves were forced to work hard for their masters. On huge farms, called plantations, they helped to plant, look after and harvest crops, such as sugar (West Indies), cotton (North America), tobacco (North and South America) and coffee (South America).

A slave would be expected to work for most of his or her life. Three- and four-year-olds would work in 'trash gangs' (weeding) or as water can carriers. Between the ages of nine and twelve, they would start to work in the fields with the adults. As they got older, slaves would often do less exhausting jobs, such as gardening, horse and carriage driving, cooking, cleaning or nursing. However, hard work, poor diet, tough punishments and no proper medical attention meant that few slaves lived to any great age. Shockingly, the average life expectancy for a slave was 26.

▾ **Source B** A slave's day

5:30am	– Go straight to fields. Take breakfast with you. Work until 8:00am. Latecomers are whipped.
8:00am	– Stop work for breakfast: boiled **yam** and **okra** seasoned with salt and pepper.
8:30am	– Continue with work.
12:00pm	– Rest and lunch: salted meat or pickled fish.
2:00pm	– Start work again.
6:00pm	– Return to huts.
Night time	– During the harvest season, work in the mill or boiling houses through the night.

▾ **Source A** A sugar plantation in the West Indies, 1823. Paintings like this would hang in the homes of proud plantation owners.

Slaves had no legal rights. They weren't allowed to learn to read or write, marry or own property. As you might imagine, some slaves tried to run away, but this was a very risky business in case they were caught. Special teams of 'runaway hunters' scoured the countryside looking for them. Any runaway slaves were severely punished (see **Sources C** and **D**).

▾ **Source C** Based on a report by a visitor to a plantation

PUNISHMENTS FOR SLAVES WHO BREAK MY LAWS.

For any rebellions: rebels nailed to the ground then burnt; fire applied starting at the feet, gradually moving up to the head.

For continued running away: removal of hand, foot or testicles with an axe.

For running away: neck ring or iron **muzzle**.

Failing to do duties properly: lashed for every year of the slave's life.

R Kennedy, plantation owner, Jamaica 1767

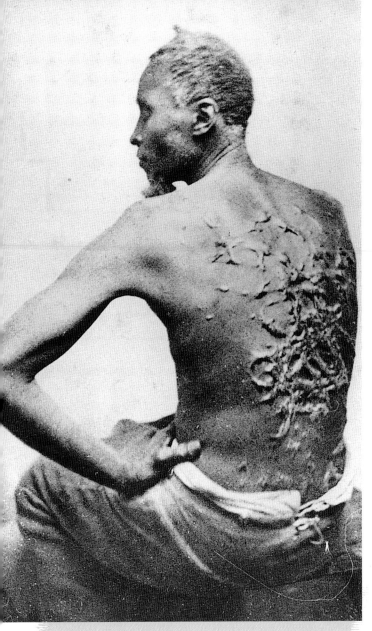

▲ **Source D** A photograph of an escaped slave named Gordon

▼ **Source E** A copy of a reward poster for an escaped slave. Although it was dangerous, thousands of slaves fled to states in the US that had already freed the slaves.

$150 REWARD

RUNAWAY SLAVE – left on the night of the 2nd
A negro man, who calls himself HENRY MAY, about 22 years old, 5 feet 6 or 8 inches tall, ordinary colour, chunky build, bushy head and has it divided mostly on one side, keeps it very nicely combed, has been raised in the house and is a first-rate dining room servant. Worked in a tavern in Louisville for 18 months. I expect he has gone back there. He may try to get employment on a steamboat. He is a good cook and is very handy. When he left, he was wearing a dark red coat, dark red pants [trousers], new – he had other clothes too. ·
50 dollar reward if taken in Louisville, 100 dollars if taken one hundred miles from Louisville but still in this state, and 150 dollars if taken out of this state, and delivered to me, or secured in jail so that I can use him again.

WILLIAM BURKE

Bardstown, Kentucky, 3 September, 1838

Some slaves joined together and started rebellions. In 1791, a **revolt** started on the island of St Dominique in the West Indies. The slaves, led by a man called Toussant L'Ouveture, set fire to the sugar cane fields and murdered their white masters. First, they defeated British troops sent to sort out the trouble … and then a French army. In 1800, the 'free' slaves renamed their island. They called it Haiti. This was the first island run by former black slaves in the West Indies. Perhaps others would follow…

 WISE UP WORDS

revolt   yam   lashed   okra   muzzle

WORK

1 a What was the attitude of the slave owners towards their slaves?
   b Why do you think many slave owners treated their slaves so brutally, especially when they tried to escape?
   c As a slave, write a diary entry of NO MORE than 250 words, describing a day in your life.

2 Look at **Source A**.
   a Describe what it shows.
   b The working conditions in this picture don't appear to be that bad. What could explain this?

3 Look at **Source E**.
   a Why were advertisements like this produced?
   b Why do you think the owner believes the runaway will look for a job on a steamboat?
   c The owner asks that this slave is returned so that he 'can use him again'. What is the owner worried about? Look at **Sources C** and **D** before writing your answer.

4 a What effect do you think the revolt in St Dominique would have had on slave owners in other countries? Explain your answer carefully.
   b Why do you think Haiti is a very special island to many black Africans, even today?

Why was slavery abolished?

AIMS

▶ What were some of the attitudes towards black Africans in the 1800s?
▶ Who were some of the key figures in the fight to end slavery?

Before beginning this page, use a dictionary to look up the word '**abolish**'. In 1833, slavery was abolished in the British Empire. These pages examine why.

Ordinary people didn't know much about black Africans. For many years, they had heard stories that they were savage **cannibals** who could barely talk. They believed Africans lived in trees and were not capable of feeling any emotion, including love. To many British people of the time, it didn't matter that these sorts of people were slaves. After all, as slaves, they would be taught to be good Christians so that would make them into better human beings.

▼ **Source A** Adapted from 'The races of Men', by Dr Robert Knox, 1850

'Look at the Negro, so well known to you. Is he shaped like any white person? Is the anatomy of his frame of his muscles, or organs like ours? Does he walk like us? Not in the least. What a hatred the white people have for him. Can the blacks become civilised? I should say not.'

▼ **Source B** Written by a Frenchman in the eighteenth century

'Africans are not human. If we say that they are human, people will say that we are not Christians.'

▼ **Source C** Written by a Scottish lawyer in 1790

'God says that slavery is right, so it is wrong to stop it. It makes the African happy, so it would be cruel to end it.'

However, not everyone had the same attitude as the writers of **Sources A, B** and **C**. Some knew that the slave trade was cruel and immoral and worked hard to end it. These people had a desire to help other human beings who were less fortunate than themselves. Others had first hand experience. They were former slaves now living in Britain who wanted to make people aware of how terribly the slaves were treated.

Look at the following fact boxes carefully. They give details of some of the key figures in the fight against the slave trade.

Fact 1: ▶

Granville Sharp – Chairman of the Society for the Abolition of the Slave Trade

• Sharp helped slaves in court. He defended men who had committed no criminal act so they could not be removed from England.

• Sharp fought many cases. He not only saved dozens of slaves from being sent back to the plantations, but also, through his court cases, made people aware of the part Britain played in the terrible slave trade.

Fact 2: ▶

William Wilberforce – MP and committed Christian

• Wilberforce organised huge **petitions** against slavery and made passionate speeches in Parliament. He was helped by his friend, Thomas Clarkson, who visited slave ships, talked to the sailors and even collected objects such as whips, chains, handcuffs and thumbscrews, which were used to punish slaves.

Fact 3: ▶

Olaudah Equiano

- Equiano, formerly a slave, managed to buy his freedom (some owners allowed their slaves to earn some money; if they saved hard they could sometimes save enough to buy themselves!).
- In 1789, he wrote his life story, detailing all the terrible things that happened to him while he was a slave, taken from Africa at the age of ten.
- His book became a best-seller and turned many people against slavery.

Fact 4: ▶

Josiah Wedgwood

- Wedgwood was a leading pottery maker who designed and gave away 200 000 medals, plates and seals in an attempt to show people his disgust in the slave trade. The words on the seal say: 'Am I not a man and a brother?'

▼ This seal contains the slogan of the Society for the Abolition of the Slave Trade.

 WISE UP WORDS

cannibals   petitions   abolish

The campaign against slavery eventually worked. Thousands of meetings, books, petitions, posters, cartoons, poems and letters to newspapers over the course of many years had an effect. In 1807, Parliament made it illegal for any British person to buy or sell another human being. This meant that no more slaves could be taken from Africa in British ships, but this did not give freedom to slaves already working in the plantations. Eventually, in 1833, Parliament decided to abolish slavery altogether. Other nations, such as America, followed British example soon after.

WORK

1   Write a sentence or two to explain the word 'abolish'.

2   Look at **Sources A**, **B** and **C**.
   a   Make a list of all the politically incorrect attitudes you can find in the sources.
   b   Do you think these attitudes explain the way slaves were treated? Explain your answer carefully.
   c   What evidence is there on these pages that not all white people thought of black Africans in this way?

3   a   Write a sentence or two about the role played in the abolition of slavery by the following people:
      i) Granville Sharp
      ii) William Wilberforce
      iii) Thomas Clarkson
      iv) Olaudah Equiano
      v) Josiah Wedgwood
   b   In your opinion, who do you think was most important? Give reasons for your answer.

4   Imagine you are a newspaper journalist in 1800. You work for one of the growing number of newspapers that are slowly turning against the idea of slavery. Your editor has asked you to compile a 'news exclusive' called 'SLAVERY – THE REAL STORY'.
   - Write one article about the slave trade itself – how does the 'slave triangle' operate?
   - Write one about conditions on board a slave ship – why do so many slaves die?
   - Write another about the sale of slaves and the work on the plantations – what work did slaves do and why were they punished so severely?
   - Also write about the campaign to end slavery – who are the key figures?
   - Include appropriate pictures and quotes.

Have you been learning?

Task 1

A homophone is a word that sounds the same as another word, but has a different meaning and spelling. For example, a sale in the shops and a sail on a ship. The words sound the same but they are not spelt the same.

a Copy the sentences below, writing the correct words from the choices in brackets:

i) In 1750, most goods were (scent/sent) from one (plaice/place) to another by (road/rowed). This took a long (time/thyme). (By/Buy) 1900, the railways had speeded up the process and had become the (main/maine) method of transporting goods around Britain.

ii) (There/Their) were (sum/some) (foul/fowl) factory towns in Victorian Britain. Litter and human (waist/waste) were just (throne/thrown) into the streets and most toilets were little more than a (whole/hole) in the ground.

iii) (They're/There/Their) was (no/know) proper police force before 1829. Then Robert Peel set up Britain's first Metropolitan Police Force in London (in/inn) response (to/two) the growing crime rate. It was a (great/grate) success and the 'boys in (blew/blue)' have (bean/been) patrolling (hour/our) streets ever since.

b Try making up your own sentences that are full of homophones. Base them on your knowledge and understanding of your history lesson.

Task 2

Here are eight groups of words and phrases. In each group, there is an odd one out. When you think you have found it, write a sentence or two explaining why you think it doesn't fit in with the others.

a post box • sewing machine • bicycle • microwave oven

b typhoid • cholera • AIDS • smallpox

c transportation • sheep stealing • murder • coining

d peelers • bobbies • Sir Robert Peel • evil blue devils

e Mary Ann Nichols • Annie Chapman • Dr Thomas Cream • Elizabeth Stride

f Australia • France • New Zealand • India

g factory owner • doctor • lawyer • miner

h truncheon • handcuffs • rattle • gun

Task 3

A poster advertising a slave auction. The word 'griffe' means mixed race.

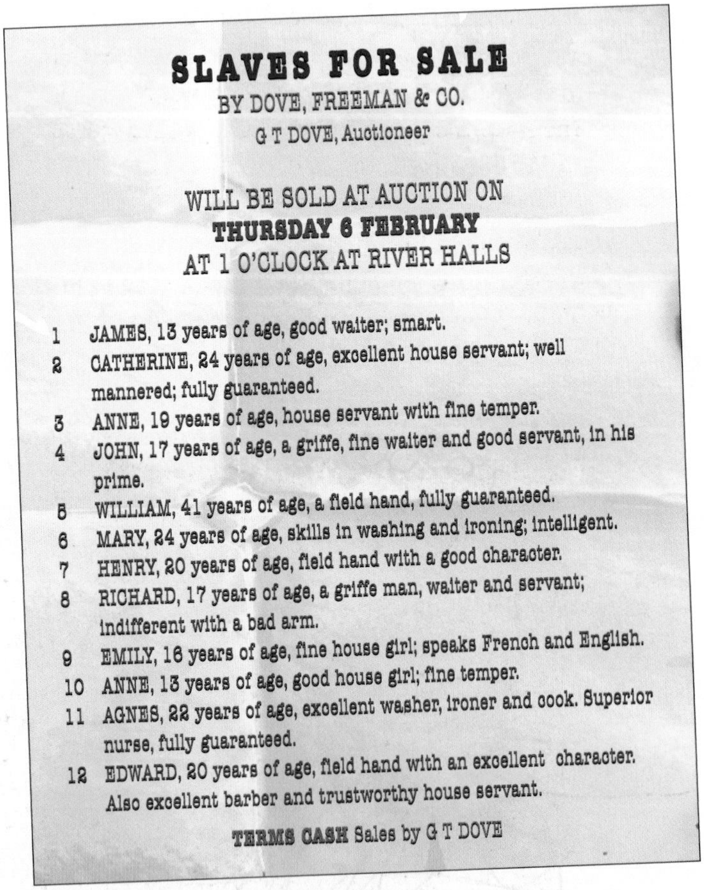

SLAVES FOR SALE
BY DOVE, FREEMAN & CO.
G T DOVE, Auctioneer

WILL BE SOLD AT AUCTION ON
THURSDAY 6 FEBRUARY
AT 1 O'CLOCK AT RIVER HALLS

1   JAMES, 13 years of age, good waiter; smart.
2   CATHERINE, 24 years of age, excellent house servant; well mannered; fully guaranteed.
3   ANNE, 19 years of age, house servant with fine temper.
4   JOHN, 17 years of age, a griffe, fine waiter and good servant, in his prime.
5   WILLIAM, 41 years of age, a field hand, fully guaranteed.
6   MARY, 24 years of age, skills in washing and ironing; intelligent.
7   HENRY, 20 years of age, field hand with a good character.
8   RICHARD, 17 years of age, a griffe man, waiter and servant; indifferent with a bad arm.
9   EMILY, 16 years of age, fine house girl; speaks French and English.
10 ANNE, 13 years of age, good house girl; fine temper.
11 AGNES, 22 years of age, excellent washer, ironer and cook. Superior nurse, fully guaranteed.
12 EDWARD, 20 years of age, field hand with an excellent character. Also excellent barber and trustworthy house servant.

TERMS CASH Sales by G T DOVE

a Read the poster carefully. Describe what a 'slave auction' was.

b What other way could slaves be sold?

c Which slaves do you think fetched the highest price at this auction? Give reasons for your answer.

d Which slaves (or slave) do you think was sold for the cheapest price? Give reasons for your answer.

e This is what a priest told slaves who were about to be auctioned in 1806:

'Your bodies, you know, are not your own; they are at the disposal of those you belong to.'

What do you think the priest meant?

Task 4

This is a very famous drawing by an artist called William Hogarth. It was drawn in 1751 and is called *Gin Lane*. It shows the dangers of drinking cheap gin, a drink that was readily available between 1750 and 1850.

Look for:

i) the drunk mother dropping her baby;

ii) the dead alcoholic whose dog is sitting next to him;

iii) the entrances to two pubs, shown by gin tankards hanging over the doors;

iv) the desperate (and poor) man and woman trying to sell their pots and pans to get money for gin. The shop is a pawnbroker's and people would sell their goods during the week and buy them back when they were paid!

v) gin being fed to a baby;

vi) the drunk men playing around in a wheelbarrow;

vii) the dead man being lowered into his coffin – what do you think has caused his death?

viii) the dead man hanging by a rope inside his house – was it suicide perhaps? If so, why might he have killed himself?

ix) the house about to fall on those below – was money spent on gin rather than repairs?

x) the man sharing his bone with a dog – is he too poor to eat properly … or is he too drunk to care?

a Why do you think Hogarth drew this picture?

b Do you think it got the message across about the dangers of drinking gin? Explain your answer carefully.

c Imagine you have been given the job of writing about the drawing for inclusion in a gallery's guidebook. Write a short description of *Gin Lane*. Include facts and figures about the drawing (artist, date, topic) and several features to look out for. You <u>must not</u> use more than 150 words!

1848: how close was a British revolution?

AIMS

▸ How did people try to fight for their rights in the 1800s?
▸ Who were the Chartists and what did they want?
▸ What did the Chartists achieve?

On 10 April 1848, a huge meeting was planned at Kennington Common, South London. Half a million angry people were expected to attend. They wanted change. After the **rally**, the people were going to march to Parliament and present a petition containing six million signatures, outlining their demands. Fergus O'Connor, a man who was due to speak at the rally, had even published new plans for running the country – with him as the new President!

▲ **Source A** The Kennington Common Rally, April 1848

As you might expect, the Government saw this as a threat. They thought it might be the start of a revolution, similar to others that had happened in other countries. Queen Victoria was moved out of London to the safety of the Isle of Wight. 150 000 new policemen were signed up and 100 000 heavily-armed soldiers were brought in to protect the city. The old war hero, the Duke of Wellington, was put in charge of London's defences and immediately took over the railways and telegraph services.

But what was the rally all about? What changes did the people want? Were they successful? And how close did Britain really come to revolution in the spring of 1848?

Today, as much as ever, people complain about the way the Government runs the country. You rarely watch a news or current affairs programme without some discussion about tax rises, hospital waiting lists, the criminal justice system or the state of Britain's schools (watch the news tonight and find out!).

In 1750, many people complained about issues that concerned them – living and working conditions, rising prices and voting rights. Sometimes, groups of unhappy people joined together to protest – sometimes peacefully, but often violently. In fact, between 1750 and 1840, there were over 700 full-scale riots in Britain!

Read the three fact boxes carefully. They outline some of the more famous riots and protests. For each one, make sure you understand what the protesters wanted and whether or not their actions had any effect.

Fact box No. 1: ▶ The Luddites

Some workers were upset that new factory machinery could do the work that maybe ten men used to do. These men formed gangs and went around smashing up the new machinery. In 1811, the machine-smashers, or Luddites as they became known, destroyed machines in the Midlands, Yorkshire and Lancashire. They were led by a man called Ned Ludd who lived secretly in Sherwood Forest, Nottingham – but no one ever found him (perhaps he never *really* existed).

The gangs caused thousands of pounds worth of damage – and the Government took strict action. Machine-smashing became a crime punishable by death.

Fact box No. 2: ▶ The 'Swing' Riots

In 1830, the machine-smashers reappeared. This time, workers in the countryside attacked farm machinery because farmers began to use machines to do the work that men used to do.

Fields were set on fire, farmhouses were burned down and barns smashed up. Farmers received threatening letters, often signed by 'Captain Swing', the leader of the rioters (it is unlikely he ever existed any more than Ned Ludd did!).

Again, the Government took tough action. Nineteen people were hanged, 644 put in prison and 481 were transported to Australia. Despite the riots, farmers continued to use the new machinery and many farm workers left the countryside to look for work in the towns and cities.

Fact box No. 3: ▶ The 'Peterloo'

For many hundreds of years, only a small number of men (rich ones) had been allowed to vote in elections. Many ordinary people, who couldn't vote, felt this was unfair. They thought that MPs would listen more closely to their complaints about their lives if they were voters. In August 1819, a huge, non-violent meeting was held in St Peter's Field, Manchester. Thousands of men, women and children attended carrying banners demanding 'Votes for All'. However, things soon got out of hand.

The Government sent in soldiers to arrest the speakers and break up the crowd. But the sword-waving soldiers managed to kill 11 people and injure 400 more. The youngest victim was a baby, William Fildes, who was knocked out of his mother's arms and trampled to death by horses.

WORK

1 a What did Luddites and Swing Rioters have in common?

   b In what ways were they different?

2 Why do you think they both failed?

3 Why were Ned Ludd and Captain Swing never caught?

Source B People soon called the massacre 'Peterloo', a sarcastic reference to the famous Battle of Waterloo, when British soldiers defeated the French in 1815.

FACT: ▶ Rules, rules, rules!

ELECTION RULES, 1830

- No man under 21 can vote ... and no women at all!

- Only men who own property worth 40 shillings per year (if they were to rent it out) can vote.

- Voting is not secret … you have to announce who you're voting for.

- Each man standing for election is called a **candidate**. The candidate with most votes becomes the Member of Parliament (**MP**) for that area … and you're not paid to do the job.

- As an MP, you will probably belong to one of the two main political parties – the **Whigs** or the **Tories**. The Whigs feel that some changes are needed to the voting system (and Britain in general), whilst the Tories don't want any changes at all.

- The political party which has the most MPs forms the Government and its leader becomes Prime Minister (PM). The Government makes the laws. The king or queen doesn't interfere too much so running Britain is left up to the PM and his MPs.

This is how democracy worked in Britain in 1830. Does any part of it seem unfair or just plain wrong?

As you have probably worked out, one of the hottest issues in Britain in the 1800s was the right to vote. Increasing numbers of ordinary people wanted to choose their leaders by voting for them in elections. This system of choosing leaders through voting is known as **democracy**.

PAUSE FOR THOUGHT

As a class, discuss what is meant by the word 'democracy'.

At the beginning of the 1800s, Britain was a sort of democracy. There were elections to choose people to run the country, but only those who owned valuable property were allowed to vote. This meant that in 1831, out of a population of about 20 million people, only 450 000 were rich enough to vote – and choose the people to run the lives of the rest. Poorer people thought this was unfair – if they had the right to vote, perhaps they might be able to 'vote in' MPs who would improve their lives!

The election in **Source C**, typical of one in the early 1800s, was a poor way to find people to run the country. Clearly there were problems with Britain's democracy. There was no secret voting and people were bribed to vote by those who wanted to become MPs. Also, some places (called 'rotten boroughs') only had a couple of voters (Appleby in Cumbria had one voter!), yet still sent an MP to Parliament to help run Britain.

By 1832, some MPs feared that a revolution was near. They worried that a group of rioters might become strong enough to take over the country by force and remove those currently in power. These MPs realised that change was essential and introduced modifications to the system of voting.

The 'Great' Reform Act was a huge disappointment for many ordinary working men. They wanted the vote but still didn't get it. Yes, the changes were a move in the right direction, but still four out of five men had no rights over their country. In 1836, a new campaign group was formed. Most members of this group simply wanted more change – but others wanted to take over the country and change it by force.

The Government soon saw these men as a massive threat – they were known as the Chartists.

◀ **Source C** The Election by William Hogarth. Can you see:

i) the rich men being brought in on their carriages to vote?

ii) one of the voters (underneath the blue flag) being told how to vote?

iii) two thugs dragging a sick man to the election so he can vote?

The Reform Act, 1832

- number of voters increased to about 800 000
- gave some big, new industrial towns, like Manchester, MPs for the first time
- some of the old 'rotten boroughs' removed

The changes made in 1832 are often called the 'Great Reform Act' by historians. But was it so great? Still only one in five men could vote … and no women! You still had to own property to vote and there were still some rotten boroughs. And voting still wasn't secret – which led to the problems encountered in **Source D**.

▼ **Source D** An account of an election in Wolverhampton in 1835

'Everybody was told that if they voted **against** Colonel Anson they would be in trouble, if they voted **for** him they were greeted with loud cheers. If they voted for Sir Goodricke they were hissed, booed and spat on. One voter had a load of horse dung thrown all over him and dead birds were thrown at another.'

WORK

1. Look at **Source B**.
   a. What did the St Peter's Field demonstrators want?
   b. What sort of people went to the demonstration that day?
   c. Why do you think the Government reacted so violently to the demonstration?
   d. How does the artist show the Government had no sympathy for the people at St Peter's Field?
   e. Whose side was the artist on? Explain your answer.

2. Explain what is happening in **Source C**. Refer to as many details in the painting as possible.

3. a. Using these two pages, make a list of things that were either wrong or unfair about the voting system before 1832.
   b. Can you think of any new voting rules that could be introduced to stop some of the problems you've noted in your answer to a?

4. a. What percentage of people were allowed to vote before and after 1832? (Use a calculator!)
   b. What is your opinion of the Reform Act of 1832? Is it right that some historians call it the 'Great' Reform Act? Explain your opinions carefully.

The Chartists – reformers or revolutionaries?

In 1838, a meeting was held in Birmingham to draw up a list of desirable changes to the voting system in Britain. Ordinary working people attended the meeting – printers, shopkeepers, tailors, carpenters, shoemakers, newsagents and factory workers. The meeting agreed on six demands and the list was called **the People's Charter**. Those who agreed with the 'Charter' became known as **Chartists**.

> ▼ **Source E** This is what the Chartists wanted. They discussed the possibility of including 'votes for women' but decided this was a step too far!

The six points of the PEOPLE'S CHARTER

1. **Every man of 21 years of age or over should be allowed to vote.**

2. **Voting should be done in secret. This would stop bribery.**

3. **Anyone should be allowed to become an MP, not only those who own property.**

4. **MPs should be paid and then ordinary people could afford to become MPs.**

5. **Voting districts (constituencies) should have an equal number of voters.**

6. **There should be an election every year.**

All Chartists wanted change. They saw that many rich people in Britain were getting even richer, but most workers remained poor ... and lived in horrible conditions. They wanted the Government to help them, but believed they didn't care! Some workers even lost their jobs because new machinery replaced them. They felt that very little was done to help them because there was no one to speak up for them. The Charter would be their attempt to make the voting system fairer – and open to all (except women – maybe later!). If working men had the vote, they could elect MPs who promised to look after them!

For the Chartists, persuading Parliament to adopt their ideas was the difficult part. They held huge rallies in big cities such as Birmingham, Liverpool and Leeds, hoping to attract support and show the Government that a huge number of people agreed with them. Then, in 1839, they drew up a **petition**, signed by over one million people (it was three miles long!) who supported the Chartists' ideas. The petition was sent to Parliament so that MPs could see how many people wanted the changes.

Parliament ignored the petition when it arrived at their door. So another petition was organised, this time containing three million signatures. Yet again, Parliament ignored it. Some Chartist leaders started to get angry at Parliament's refusal to listen. Some talked about revolution, taking the country over and forcing the changes. Others continued to encourage the old-fashioned, peaceful methods. Read **Sources F** and **G** carefully. Try to work out which one of the leaders wants to use force and which one wants to remain peaceful.

> ▼ **Source F** From a speech by William Lovell, one of the Chartist leaders

'Let us, friends, seek to join together the honest moral, hard-working and intelligent members of society. Let us find out about our rights from books. Let us collect information about our lives, our wages and our conditions. Then let us publish our views. Then MPs will agree there must be change, without having to use violence or arrest.'

> ▼ **Source G** From a speech made by Fergus O'Connor, another Chartist leader

'I do not want to use force, but if we do not succeed we must use violence. It is better to die free men than live as slaves. Violence is the right thing to do if it wins us our freedom.'

In 1848, a third petition was organised. This one had over six million signatures! The Chartists planned a huge meeting of half a million Chartists on Kennington Common, South London, before marching to Parliament with their demands.

The Government was worried – was this the start of a revolution? Plans were drawn up to defend London and Queen Victoria was moved to safety. But the meeting was a huge flop! It rained heavily and only 20 000 Chartists turned up (see **Source A**). That's right – a possible revolution failed because of bad weather!

The petition turned into a bit of a flop too. When Parliament inspected the petition, it was found to contain fewer than two million names – and many of them were fake. Queen Victoria herself was supposed to have signed it ten times, as well as 'April First', 'Cheeky the Marine', 'No Cheese', 'Pugnose', 'Flat nose', 'Long nose' and 'Mr Punch'.

After their dramatic failure in 1848, little was heard of the Chartists again. They had failed … or had they?

A success story?

The Chartists were the first organised national protest movement. They drew attention to the problems and frustrations of working people and showed that there were national issues that the Government must pay attention to. In fact, of their six original demands, all but one (point 6) later became law.

For a few brief days in the spring of 1848, the Government feared the Chartists. How does Britain really come to revolution is open for discussion, but the Chartists showed that the working class was a powerful and potentially threatening force that must be **pacified** in the future.

▼ **Source H** From J D Clare's 'Investigating History, 1750–1900'

'In 1867, the Second Reform Act gave the vote to every man who had a house, and in 1884, the Third Reform Act gave the vote to every British man who was not mad, a criminal, or a lord. In 1872, the Ballot Act said that people had to vote in secret by putting their ballot paper in a ballot box. This stopped people bribing or bullying voters into voting for them.'

WISE UP WORDS

rally   democracy   petition   Chartists   candidate   Whigs   MP   the People's Charter   ballot   Tories   pacify

WORK

1 a Who were the Chartists?
   b List their six demands.
   c Pick two that you think were most important to the workers. Give reasons for your choices.
   d Which of the six demands is not in force today?
   e Can you think why this has never been made law?

2 Look at **Sources F** and **G**.
   a Rewrite each source in your own words.
   b Write a sentence to explain these two words:
      reformer • revolutionary
   c In your opinion, who was the reformer and who was the revolutionary? Give reasons for your decision.

3 Write an essay that answers the question, 'Were the Chartists a success or not?' Organise your essay into short paragraphs:
   • What changes did the Chartists want?
   • Why did working people join them?
   • How did they try to get change?
   • What had they achieved by 1850?
   • Were they a long-term success, rather than a short-term one?

TOP TIP: Your essay title is a question – make sure you answer it!

Sexist Britain?

AIMS

▶ How did women's rights differ from men's?

▶ How had women's rights begun to change by 1900?

In 1832, Joseph Thomson tried to sell his wife at auction for 50 shillings (£2.50). He told buyers (**Source A**):

▼ **Source A**

'Gentlemen, I offer my wife, Mary Anne Thomson, whom I mean to sell to the highest bidder. It is her wish as well as mine to part forever. She has been a snake to me. I took her for my comfort but she has turned into a curse, a tormentor and a daily devil. However, she has a bright and sunny side. She can read novels, milk cows, make butter and shout at our maid. She cannot make rum, gin or whisky, but she is a good judge from long experience in tasting them.'

Unbelievably, Mr Thomson managed to sell his wife for 20 shillings (£1.00) and a dog! Today, we are shocked by the actions of this man. In fact, what Mr Thomson did is now against the law, but in 1832, it wasn't. Mr Thomson was simply treating his wife as his property – and he was free to do whatever he wanted with her. Look through **Sources B** to **F** carefully. In today's world where men and women have equal rights under the law, it is difficult to imagine women's place in society between 1750 and 1900.

▲ **Source C** A punishment for nagging wives in 1812, 'The Ducking Stool'

▼ **Source B** From J F Aylett's 'The Suffragettes and After'

'[In 1800], once married, her husband owned her. That was the way men saw it, and in effect, that was the law of the land. A wife's duty was to obey her husband. If she did not, he could beat her. A wife's duty was to please her husband; if she did not he might take a mistress. Either way, there was almost nothing she could do about it. An Act of Parliament was necessary to end a marriage. It could cost £2 000 and only two women ever did it. It was quite different for the man. He could spend all 'her' money and she could not stop him. If he got into debt, her possessions could be taken to pay off the debts ... even her clothes!'

▼ **Source D** Adapted from what was said by Thomas Huxley, a leading scientist in the 1800s

'In every way, both mental and physical, the average woman is inferior to the average man.'

▼ **Source E** The writer W M Thackeray's thoughts on the ideal woman. Make sure you understand words such as 'exquisite' and 'humble'.

'An exquisite slave, a humble, flattering, lace-making, piano-playing being who laughs at all our jokes, however old they are, helps us and fondly lies to us throughout life.'

! WISE UP WORDS

maintenance   inferior

who split up with her husband was allowed to claim money or **maintenance** to support her and the children. In 1891, wives were no longer forced, as they had been, to stay with their husbands if they wanted to leave.

By 1900, women's rights had taken a huge step forward. But one of the most burning issues remained – women still couldn't vote in national elections; nor could they become MPs. This issue would not be resolved until the next century!

▲ **Source F** An 1851 painting by Richard Redgrave called The Outcast. Look out for:

i) the unmarried mother ii) the reaction of her family
iii) the pointing, older man – why is he pointing?

Women from all classes of society, both rich and poor, depended on men. Whilst poorer women's lives were undeniably harder (they had to work for a start), all women were second-class citizens with few rights. It was difficult for women to change this because the country was controlled by men. All the MPs were men, only men could vote in elections and they had all the important jobs.

However, this situation couldn't last and changes started to happen. In 1842, women were banned from working down mines and later they were stopped from working any more than ten hours a day in a factory.

More and more women were being educated and getting jobs as typists, teachers, nurses and shop assistants. Some women went a step further. They were brave enough to 'go it alone'. They decided that a traditional woman's life was not for them and became great role models in Victorian society. These independent women forced people around them to think again about the position women held in society.

After 1857, wives could divorce husbands who were violent to them and in 1870, they were allowed to keep any money they earned. Eight years later, any woman

WORK

1 Look at **Source A**.
   a What words does Joseph Thomson use to insult his wife?
   b What does he say are her good points?
   c How does Joseph Thomson hint that his wife drinks a lot?
   d What shocks you about **Source A**?

2 Look at **Source C**. The ducking stool was just for wives. Nagging men didn't have any similar punishment. Either describe or draw your own punishment for a man who is lazy, mean and violent or just nags a lot. Explain your punishment or invention carefully.

3 a Explain what is meant by the word 'sexist'.
   b Make a list of sexist laws, rules and regulations that were in force in Britain in the early 1800s.
   c Why do you think these laws were in force? You may want to read **Source D** again before answering.
   d How did things begin to change from 1842?
   e What very sexist law still remained in place in 1900?

4 Look at **Source E**. Imagine that W M Thackeray was to place an advertisement in a 'lonely hearts' column to meet his ideal woman. Write out the sort of advert you think he might place in a newspaper. Do you think he'd get many responses if he placed his advert today? Explain your answer carefully.

Improving working conditions

AIMS

▶ Why were some factory owners unwilling to improve working conditions?

▶ How did working conditions gradually change?

In 1800, a factory in Manchester was given a terrifying nickname. It was known as the 'Cripple Factory'. Years and years of heavy lifting, broken arms and severe beatings meant that many of the young men, women and children who worked there were crippled forever. The mines weren't much better either. One 11-year-old girl working as a coal-carrier describes her job in **Source A**. **Source B** also gives an idea of what her job entailed.

▼ **Source A** Working in a mine

'I go down the pit at two in the morning and I don't come up again until the next afternoon. I go to bed at six at night to be ready for work the next morning ... I carry coal tubs up ladders all day. Each coal tub holds 4¼ cwt [216 kilos – about as heavy as three adults] and I get beaten when I don't work hard enough.'

Today, the Government would not let this sort of thing happen. Many people in 1800 thought that politicians had no right to interfere with the working conditions in factories. They believed that it was up to the owners to decide how they ran their factories and mines. After all, they owned them, didn't they? The Government had no right to meddle in the private arrangement between a worker and an employer. It was called **laissez faire**, French words meaning 'leave alone'.

Some people argued that people might work harder if they were treated better! **Reformers** like Lord Shaftesbury, Richard Oastler, John Fieldon and Michael Sadler (another MP) began to campaign for laws to protect factory and mine workers. Protection of the children was seen as the first priority, then women and later the men.

▲ **Source B** Tough work in the mining industry

1833 FACTORY ACT
– No children under nine to work in the factories
– Nine hours work per day for children aged 9–13
– Two hours school per day
– Factory inspectors appointed (but there were only four!)

1842 MINES ACT
– No women or children under ten to work down a mine
– Mine inspectors appointed

1844 FACTORY ACT
– No women to work more than 12 hours per day
– Machines to be made safer

1847 TEN HOUR ACT
– Maximum ten-hour day for all women and workers under 18

1850 FACTORY ACT
– Machines to only operate between 6:00am and 6:00pm

1871 TRADE UNION ACT
– Trade unions made legal. Workers all doing the same job (trade) – like railway workers or dockers for example – were allowed to join together (union) to negotiate with their employers for improvements to pay and working conditions. As a last resort, all union members could go on strike!

1895 FACTORY ACT
– Children under 13 to work a maximum of 30 hours per week

▶ **Source C** New acts to protect workers

Some men collected evidence to prove how bad things were. Their findings shocked the nation.

> ▼ **Source D** A few questions and answers from the Sadler Report, an investigation into factory conditions in 1832. Dozens of workers like Matthew Crabtree were interviewed.

Interviewer: Were you sometimes late?

Matthew: Yes, and if we were even five minutes late, we were beaten black and blue by the overseer. He hit us with a strap.

Interviewer: Do you know of any accidents?

Matthew: Yes, there was a boy who got hit by a machine. He broke both legs and one of them was cut open from his knee to his waist. His head was cut, his eyes were nearly torn out and he broke both arms.

WARNING! This interview is taken from a report by an MP called Michael Sadler. Some historians think he exaggerated the answers when writing up his investigation. He wanted conditions to appear even worse than they already were. Regardless of this, the Sadler Report made a huge impact.

> ▼ **Source E** From the Mines Report of 1842. Betty Harris, aged 37, describes her work. She pulled coal along in large wagons.

'I have a belt around my waist and I go on my hands and feet ... the belt and chain are worse when we are in the family way [pregnant]. I've had three or four children born on the same days as I have been at work and have gone back to work nine or ten days later. Four out of my eight children were still-born.'

After reading the reports, Parliament acted. From 1833, new laws or **Acts** made great changes to the working lives of women and children. Men, it was believed, could look after themselves.

Some factory owners hated the changes. They felt politicians had no right to meddle in their business and thought of ways to avoid keeping to the new rules. But the new laws kept coming and, gradually, they began to protect more and more workers. Inspectors were even appointed to enforce them!

By 1900, factories and mines had become safer and more bearable. They still weren't particularly pleasant places to work, but Parliament had accepted that they had a duty to look after the more vulnerable people in society.

FACT: ▶ Were all bosses bad?

▶ Some factory owners had been trying to help their workers for years. Robert Owen built quality houses, schools, shops with cheap goods for sale, galleries and parks for his workers in Scotland. He even reduced working hours. He believed that happy workers made hard workers – and he was rewarded with huge profits!

WISE UP WORDS

reformers   laissez faire   Acts   trade union

WORK

1 a How did the 'Cripple Factory' get its terrifying nickname?
   b In your opinion, were the mines just as bad as some factories? Support your answer using evidence from some of the sources.

2 a Explain what is meant by the term 'laissez faire'.
   b Why did some factory owners believe in 'laissez faire'?
   c Explain the word 'reformer'.
   d How did the reformers bring about changes to working conditions?
   e Did all factories need reforming? Explain your answer carefully.

3 Look at **Source C**.
   a Write down three of the most important changes to working conditions between 1830 and 1895.
   b Next to each one, explain why you think it was an important change.

4 Look at **Source D**.
   a Write down three words or phrases that a reader of this report might feel.
   b Why might this interview NOT be totally reliable? Give reasons for your answer.
   c Do any of Matthew's answers seem a bit exaggerated? Explain your answer.
   d How could a historian get a more reliable view of factory life in the 1800s? You might want to discuss this question with your classmates or teacher.

Discovering the cause of cholera

AIMS

▶ How serious were the cholera outbreaks?
▶ Who discovered the cause of cholera?

London 1848 – cholera was back! Victims were violently sick and suffered from painful diarrhoea; their skin and nails turned black and blue before they fell into a coma and died. So many people were dying that cemeteries had to be closed because they were too full – bodies had started to poke through the earth's surface, letting off a disgusting stench!

Cholera had struck before in 1831, when over 50 000 people had died. A vicar in Bilston had written at the time that 'coffins could not be made fast enough for the dead'. But the epidemic passed. The deaths from cholera stopped and life gradually returned to normal. Perhaps cholera would never return!

But now cholera was back – and killing more than ever! What was causing it? And what on earth could be done to stop it?

THE APPEARANCE AFTER DEATH OF A VICTIM TO THE INDIAN CHOLERA

▲ **Source A** A cholera victim from Sunderland

In 1848, there were two main theories about the cause of cholera.

The '**Miasmatist**' – miasma means 'dirty air'. Some doctors believed that cholera was carried through the air, like a poisonous gas or an infectious mist. They thought that the air from the filthy towns caused the miasma.

The '**Contagionist**' – **contagious** means 'passed on by touch'. Some doctors thought that cholera was spread by personal contact with a sick person, their clothes or bedding.

By the disease-ridden summer of 1848, the 'miasmatists' seemed to be winning the argument over the cause of cholera. They were supported by a report on living conditions, written by Edwin Chadwick, which blamed the high death rate on, among other things, dirty air or miasma.

▼ **Source B** Part of Chadwick's report, 1842

'The diseases are caused by dirty air produced by rotting animals and vegetables, by damp and filth and close, overcrowded houses ... the loss of life from filth and bad ventilation is greater than the loss from death or wounds in any wars in which this country has taken part in recent times.'

When cholera reappeared in 1848 and killed over 60 000 people, Parliament eventually decided to take action ... the first ever **Public Health Act** was born.

The Act gave local town councils the power to spend money on cleaning up their towns if they wanted to. Some towns, like Liverpool and Birmingham, made huge improvements, but many others didn't bother to do anything.

By 1849, cholera had disappeared again and many councils felt they didn't need to waste money cleaning up their towns.

Source C Liverpool Council worked hard to clean up its city.

LIVERPOOL HEALTH COMMITTEE 1849

We undertake the following:

- **Improve toilets**
- **Remove the piles of human waste or cesspools**
- **Close down any factories that pollute the areas near homes**
- **Remove slaughterhouses**
- **Supply lots of clean water**
- **Widen the streets**

But cholera didn't stay away for long. In 1854, it killed over 20 000 people. A doctor called John Snow decided to work out once and for all what on earth kept causing it. He chose an area of London called Soho to investigate, a place where within a few streets, over 700 people had died.

Dr Snow found out that all victims in this small area got their water from the Broad Street water pump. Those who didn't die seemed to be getting their water from other places. Dr Snow asked permission to remove the handle of the water pump so people were forced to use another. There were no more deaths. Snow investigated further and found out that a street toilet, only one metre from the pump, had a cracked lining and this allowed filthy water to trickle into the drinking water.

Source D Urghh!

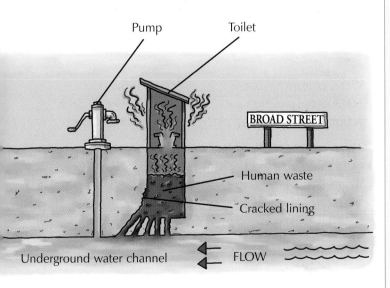

Snow had proved the 'contagionists' right. Cholera was not carried through the air like a poisonous gas or an infection mist; instead, it was caught through 'contagion', by coming into personal contact with a cholera sufferer or in this case, drinking some water contaminated by a victim's diarrhoea.

By the 1850s, the Government seemed to have a growing batch of evidence about the terrible state of the nation's health within these dirty, overcrowded towns. They even had the medical evidence that made the link between cholera, the nation's scariest disease, and water supply. So what did they do about it?

WISE UP WORDS

miasmatist   contagionist   contagious
Public Health Act

WORK

1 Look at **Source A**.
   a Describe what would have happened to this victim in the days leading up to her death.
   b Why was cholera becoming a major problem for town councils?

2 a Explain how a miasmatist thinks diseases like cholera spread.
   b In what way does a contagionist think differently?
   c Was Chadwick a miasmatist or a contagionist? Explain your answer, referring to details in **Source B** when you write.

3 Look at **Source C**.
   a Why was the 1848 Public Health Act so important?
   b Do you think the measures introduced in Liverpool would please the miasmatists, the contagionists, or both? Give reasons for your answer.

4 Make up a conversation between Dr John Snow and Edwin Chadwick. Snow is trying to convince Chadwick that his theories are correct … and Chadwick's are wrong! Think about:
   - What Snow believed to be the cause of cholera.
   - How he proved it through his investigation.
   - How Chadwick might respond.
   - How Snow could prove it once and for all.

The Sewer King

AIMS
- How did the Government clean up the towns?
- Who helped to clean them?

London 1858 – human sewage, dead animals, household rubbish, horse dung, slaughterhouse waste and chemicals from factories were all dumped in the same place – the River Thames. This river water was then used for washing clothes and cooking. Raw sewage could be seen coming out of some of the 'water' pumps in the streets. Despite the fact that Dr Snow had worked out the link between cholera and a dirty water supply, the city streets still remained a breeding ground for disease.

In the summer, a heat wave caused the filthy river to stink worse than ever. The stench was so bad, the MPs in the Houses of Parliament (which are right next to the river) demanded to meet somewhere else! It is little wonder that London at this time was nicknamed the 'Great Stink' and its people were known as the 'Great Unwashed'. So what were these MPs going to do about it? The dreaded cholera was sure to come back soon.

The sewage filled River Thames and the new evidence about cholera caused such alarm that MPs turned to a man they hoped could clean things up. Three years earlier, an **engineer** called Joseph Bazalgette had drawn up plans for huge underground tunnels (or **sewers**) to collect all the waste from nearly one million homes before it had a chance to flow into the Thames. Powerful pumps would then push all the sewage along the tunnels and out towards the sea. The MPs wanted London's streets free of sewage ... quickly! In 1858, Bazalgette was told to start work immediately. He would soon earn the nickname the 'Sewer King'.

FACT: ▶ How much?

▶ The sewers cost about £3 million in 1866. That's well over £1 billion by modern standards. Most say the money was very well spent ... cholera never returned to London after Bazalgette's sewers were fully operational.

▼ **Source A** Bazalgette's sewers were finished in 1866. There were 83 miles of sewers, removing 420 million gallons of sewage a day. He used 318 million bricks ... and many of his sewers are still used below London's streets today! Bazalgette himself is pictured here, standing above the sewers with his hands on his hips.

Parliament continued its quest to clean up the streets and improve the nation's health. Many new health measures were introduced (**Source B**).

▼ **Source B**

MAKING TOWNS HEALTHIER

1866 Sanitary Act – Towns must install a proper water supply and sewage disposal system at once. Inspectors will check this has been done.

1875 Housing Act – Councils have the power to pull down the worst houses in the worst areas and build better homes.

1875 Public Health Act – Local councils must keep the pavements lit, paved and cleaned, sewers must be clean and rubbish clear from the streets. They may increase taxes to pay for this.

The effort seems to have paid off. In 1801, the average person in a British town could expect to live to the age of 30. By 1901, they would, on average, live to the age of 50!

Many town councils tried even harder. They didn't just try to improve people's health, but also their quality of life. Swimming baths, town parks, bandstands and boating lakes were built. So too were art galleries, concert halls and libraries. Magnificent town halls were built right in the town centre to demonstrate how proud the local councillors were. One famous mayor of Birmingham, Joseph Chamberlain, went so far as saying that his council 'parked, paved, assized [provided regular courts], marketed, gas and watered and improved' the centre of the city.

▼ **Source C** Street disinfecting, London, 1877. The council was certainly trying to keep the streets clean!

 WISE UP WORDS

engineer   sewer

FACT: ▶ I'm off to use the Thomas!

▶ Thomas Crapper designed some of the best flushing toilets money could buy. He started his business in Chelsea, London, in 1861. Some of his toilets flushed straight into Bazalgette's sewers. Another young businessman making money at this time was a man called George Jennings. He started a campaign to introduce street toilets called 'halting stations'. Users would pay a penny to use them – this is where the phrase 'spending a penny' comes from.

HUNGRY FOR MORE?

Town and city councils still spend vast sums of money on local improvements – parks, roads, leisure centres, playing fields, town and city centres and much more.
• What local improvements have your council made in the last few years? List where changes have taken place.
• Have they always turned out to be 'improvements'?

WORK

1 a Why was London known as the 'Great Stink' in 1858?
   b Why do you think the people of London were known as the 'Great Unwashed'?

2 a Cholera never returned to London after Bazalgette's sewers were fully operational. Have Londoners got Bazalgette to thank for this? Explain your answer.
   b An obituary is a piece of writing about the life and achievements of someone who has just died. They appear in newspapers. Complete this obituary for 'the Sewer King', who died in 1891. The first part has been done for you.

   Joseph Bazalgette
   Born: Enfield 1819 **Died:** 1891, buried in Wimbledon
   Early life: Son of a Frenchman, began career as a railway engineer.
   Appointed chief engineer in 1856 to the London Board of Works (later the London County Council).
   Career highlights:

3 a What happened to the average age of death of a person living in a British town between 1801 and 1901?
   b Why did this improvement happen? Refer to the work of Parliament and town councils in your answer.

4 a What does the phrase 'spending a penny' mean?
   b How did this phrase originate?

A healthier nation?

AIMS
▸ Why were hospitals dangerous places?
▸ How were patients' chances of survival increased?

Look at **Source A**. It is a painting from 1750. The patient is in absolute agony. Look at his face; he is being held down whilst the surgeon cuts off his leg. The poor man won't have been given any painkilling drugs – he is completely awake when the surgeon starts to slice into his skin and saw through his thighbone. It is highly unlikely that the medical equipment he is using has ever been washed either. It will be stained with the dry blood and pus from a previous patient. One well-known surgeon used to sharpen his knives on the sole of his boot before using them. And you know how filthy the streets were! What do you think the patient's chances of survival were? Why were conditions so bad? And why have they improved so much since then?

In 1750, a patient in a British hospital had two major enemies. One was the pain during the operation; the other was infection afterwards. Either could kill you! Only when these two obstacles were dealt with would it be possible to make any real medical progress. In the nineteenth century, doctors started to find the solutions to these problems … and changed the way the sick were cared for forever!

For hundreds of years, doctors and surgeons had tried to reduce a patient's pain during surgery. Getting them drunk or hitting them over the head were two of the most common methods. But in 1846, an American dentist called William Moston tried out a new idea. He put his patients to sleep for a short period of time using a gas called **ether**. It worked! The patient felt no pain during the operation, woke up 20 minutes later and went home. Anaesthetics (based on the word 'ether') were born and the idea soon caught on amongst London's surgeons. However, ether irritated patients' eyes and made them cough and vomit during operations. So, in 1847, a Scottish doctor called James Simpson tried **chloroform** as an alternative. Again, it worked, but had less of the nasty side effects of ether. Soon, chloroform became the most common anaesthetic in the land – even Queen Victoria used it in 1853 as a painkiller whilst giving birth to her son, Leopold.

The use of anaesthetic was a great step forward, but it didn't stop people dying from infections after operations. Today, we take it for granted that our hospitals and operating theatres are very, very clean, but in the early 1800s, it was a very different story. Hospitals were dirty places, where patients were all herded together whether they had a highly contagious fever or a broken arm. The operating theatres were no better. The only thing that was ever cleaned out was the sand box from under the operating table, which was used to catch a patient's blood during surgery. The cockroaches in St Thomas' hospital in London were said to be the biggest in London. They fed on dried blood and dead skin. Doctors and surgeons didn't understand the need for cleanliness because they didn't know that germs caused disease. It would take a few more famous men to solve this problem!

FACT: ▸ Record breaker

▸ In the 1840s, a famous London surgeon named Robert Liston held the world record for **amputating** a leg – two and a half minutes. Unfortunately, he worked so fast that he accidentally cut off the patient's testicles! Also, he once cut off his assistant's fingers during another operation and a spectator dropped dead with fright.

FACT: ▶ Hospitals

▸ The word 'hospital' comes from the Latin word
'hospitali', meaning 'a place for guests'. By 1750,
London had some of the finest hospitals in Europe. St
Bartholomew's was the oldest but, by this time, rich
men with a desire to do good things had donated
money to help open many others. Westminster, Guy's,
St George's Infirmary and Middlesex hospitals were all
built before 1750 and, even today, still provide
medical care to Britain's citizens.

▼ **Source A** A painting of an amputation about to
take place

WORK

1 Write a short description of the scene in **Source A**. Use
no more than 100 words.

2 Make a list of things in **Source A** that would not
happen during an operation today.

! **WISE UP WORDS**

amputate   ether   chloroform

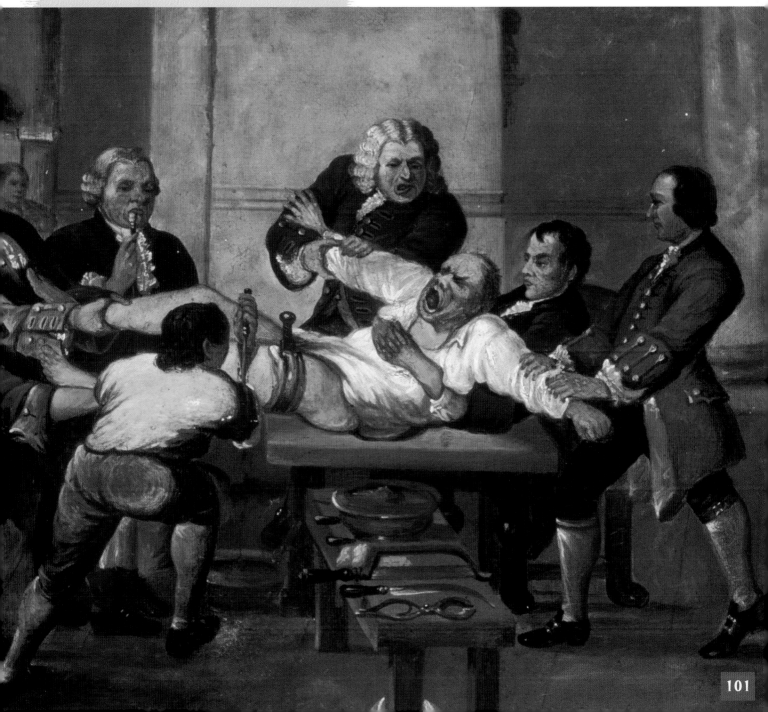

By the 1850s, surgeons were performing much better operations. As a result, the patients weren't dying of shock ... but they continued to die of blood poisoning and nasty infections instead. After all, the doctors were operating on old wooden tables, in dirty rooms, in their ordinary clothes, using unwashed instruments that had been used on several other patients that day. Many doctors just didn't realise the danger of dirt! Read **Source B** carefully.

▼ **Source B** Visiting a hospital was a risky business (adapted from J Leeson)

'A strong, young farmer came into the hospital and told the surgeon that his girlfriend had made comments about his nose – it was too much to one side; could it be straightened? He had heard of the wonderful things that were done in London hospitals. He was admitted; the septum (bone between the nostrils) was straightened and in five days he was dead. He died of hospital sepsis.'

'Sepsis' is the Greek word for 'rotten'. The farmer's wound had gone rotten and he had died from blood poisoning. In fact, the amount of patients dying after operations in the 1850s was astonishing – as many as six out of ten! In 1864, Louis Pasteur identified tiny creatures, or germs, with his microscope. He said that some of these germs caused infection and disease. This was a major breakthrough. He went on to say that many of these germs could be killed by heat – and proved it in his laboratory. We still use '**pasteurisation**' – the heating of food and drink – today (check your milk carton) to help prevent infection.

In 1867, an English doctor, Joseph Lister, took Pasteur's theories one step further. He thought that it might be germs that caused so many of his patients to die from sepsis. Surely, he believed, if the germs were killed with antiseptic ('anti' means against), then more of his patients would survive. Lister chose carbolic acid as his antiseptic. Using a pump, a bit like an aerosol can, he sprayed anything that might possibly come into contact with the wound. Spray everything, he hoped, and all the germs would die. He was right! His patient didn't get any infections and antiseptics were born.

▼ **Source C** Antiseptic in action. An operation using Lister's carbolic acid spray. Note the doctor on the left putting the patients 'to sleep' with an anaesthetic.

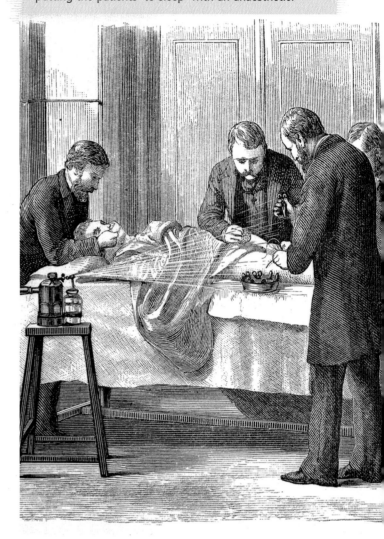

Soon doctors and surgeons all over the country were trying antiseptic sprays and other cleaner ways to work. Hospitals waged a war against germs. Walls were scrubbed clean, floors were swept and equipment was **sterilised**. Surgeons started to wear rubber gloves, surgical gowns and face masks during operations.

The results of these measures were plain to see. Hospitals started to cure more people than they killed. Astonishingly, figures from Newcastle Infirmary, published in 1878, show that before antiseptics were introduced, six out of ten people died after operations. After antiseptics, only one out of every ten died!

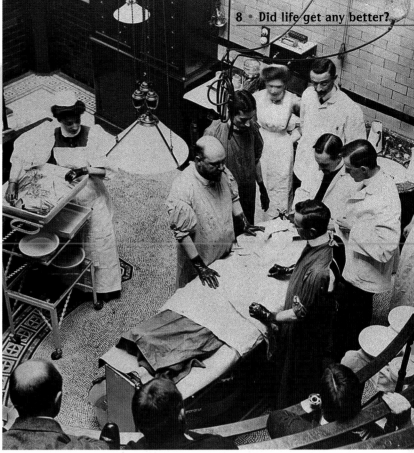

▶ **Source D** An operation in 1900. Look for all the different ways in which this surgeon tries to keep a cleaner operating room.

FACT: ▶ Vaccination

▶ In 1796, a doctor named Edward Jenner carried out a bizarre experiment. For years, he had observed that people with cowpox (a mild and harmless disease) didn't get smallpox (a serious killer disease). So he took pus from the blister of a girl who had cowpox and squirted it into two cuts in the arm of an eight-year-old boy named James Phipps. Next he injected Phipps with smallpox. It was a risky experiment but the boy didn't catch the deadly disease! Edward had discovered a way of preventing smallpox, one of Britain's biggest killers. Soon doctors were calling this method **vaccination**, from 'vacca', the Latin word for cow. By the end of 1801, over 100 000 people in Britain had been vaccinated. Soon, other doctors began to work on vaccinations for other diseases. By the 1880s, it was widely accepted that one way to prevent disease was to inject a weakened form of the germ in order to allow the body to build up its own defences. This is how it is done today.

FACT: ▶ Lister's legacy

▶ Some people called Lister a miracle worker. Perhaps you can see why!

Before Lister's antiseptic invention, out of ten people:

6 died, 4 lived after a major operation

After Lister's widespread use of antiseptic:

1 died, 9 lived after a major operation

HUNGRY FOR MORE?

Florence Nightingale is one of the most famous nurses in the world. She lived from 1820 to 1910. Find out:
- *Why she is so famous.*
- *How she changed nursing forever.*
- *Why she is called 'the lady with the lamp'.*
Use the Internet, or your school or local library.

! WISE UP WORDS

vaccination   sepsis   sterilised   pasteurisation

WORK

1 Write a sentence or two to explain the following words:
   sepsis • pasteurisation • sterilise

2 a In your own words, explain how Jenner, Simpson and Lister improved people's health. Ensure you use the words 'vaccination', 'anaesthetics' and 'antiseptic' in your answers.

   b Was one of these doctors more important than the others, or were they equally important? Give reasons for your answer.

3 Look at **Sources A** and **D**.

   a Draw two spider diagrams, each describing the main features of an operation in 1750 and 1900.

   b Compare the two diagrams and write a paragraph explaining how operations had changed between 1750 and 1900.

   c Look at your 1900 diagram and think about a modern operation. Circle the things that have changed since 1900 in one colour and underline the things that still happen today during an operation in another.

What were Victorian schools like?

AIMS
▶ How did schools change between 1750 and 1900?
▶ What was school life like for an ordinary 13-year-old pupil in Victorian Britain?

During the Victorian era, there were many investigations that looked at the way people lived and worked. Many of the investigators asked children for their opinions. As a result, we have a good view of what life was like during this time. In 1841, a group of boys told a Government enquiry that they'd never heard of London and thought the Queen's name was Albert. Few had heard of Jesus Christ either – 'Does 'e work down our pit?' asked one young miner. And these boys were being serious at the time. They could not read or write or do any simple sums. Something had to change.

By the early 1800s, some people were beginning to think that children should be taught at least some basic skills … they needed to go to proper schools.

By the 1850s, about six children in ten were getting some teaching, but the quality of that teaching was not very good! Some youngsters went to a **dame school** for an hour or more a week. Run by a local woman in the front room of her house, a child might be taught to count and say the alphabet in return for a few pennies. If this was too expensive (and for many it was), then parents could send their children to a charity or **ragged school**. First set up in 1844 for orphans and very poor children, these places often had 300 pupils in the same room with one proper teacher! 'Pupil teachers' (older boys who taught the younger ones) took lots of the lessons and, needless to say, very little learning was done.

Many children stayed away from school altogether. They were far too busy earning money by working in factories!

By the late 1860s, the Government realised that Britain needed more educated people. Engineers and scientists were needed to build and design machines. These people had to understand mathematics; mechanics needed to understand instruction manuals and secretaries and clerks needed to know how to write letters and calculate prices. Even factory workers had to be able to read notices! So in 1870, the Government introduced a new law – they said that all children from ages five to thirteen had to attend school. A few years later, they made it free!

So what was school like?

What was the timetable like?

Education was designed to equip children for life after school. There was some PE, known as 'drill' and some History and Geography too. This timetable is from a typical day at school in Bristol in 1897. Why do you think the girls and the boys learned different things?

SCHOOL TIMETABLE

Boys

Morning (9:00am–12 noon)
The three Rs = Reading, Writing and Arithmetic (done together with girls)

Afternoon (2:00pm–5:00pm)
Science, Woodwork and Technical drawing

Girls

Morning (9:00am–12 noon)
The three Rs = Reading, Writing and Arithmetic (done together with boys)

Afternoon (2:00pm–5:00pm)
Cookery, Needlework and Housework

▲ **Source A** Notice that the boys and girls have different lessons in the afternoon – can you think why?

▼ **Source B** A photograph of a Victorian schoolroom. Can you see one of the pupils asleep on the front row?

What did the schoolroom look like?

Pupils sat at wooden desks in rows, looking at a blackboard and a large map of the world. Some had walked many miles to get to the cold, draughty schoolrooms.

▲ **Source C** A lesson in housework

What were the lessons really like?

Lessons must have been pretty boring! Pupils copied from the blackboard or repeated things as a whole group. In Geography, they might list all the countries on the globe or learn all the names of the railway stations between London and Crewe. In this picture, the girls are learning how to do housework correctly – the boys would never have learned this.

PAUSE FOR THOUGHT

Why do you think that boys and girls have the same range of subjects to learn today?

How did schools keep records?

Every school had a **logbook**. It recorded everything that happened on a day-to-day basis. Carefully read the true events from Milton House School logbook and prepare to be amazed...

4 September 1879

Mr Brown was reported to have punished a boy by striking him over the head with a stick. After school had ended, Mrs Barnes called with her daughter Catherine to show an injury that Mr Brown had done to her arm by hitting her on the elbow with a stick. Mr Brown expressed deep regret and promised that such a thing should not happen again.

8 April 1881

One death during the week from fever. Every member of the Craig family ill with fever and in hospital.

6 May 1881

Margaret Luke (Class 6) died.

13 May 1881

Lots of truants. Parents told to come to school tomorrow.

25 November 1881

Sent for Mrs Ferguson. Ordered her to take home her daughter and clean her head, which is overrun with lice. This has not been noticed until now as she had a bandage over her head.

25 December 1881

School as normal.

▲ **Source D** A Victorian school's logbook

What about naughty children?

Teachers were tough – and so were punishments. Being rude, leaving school without permission, sulking, answering back, throwing ink and being late were all punishable offences.

> ▼ **Source E** The following punishments were all used in British schools.

1. the cane

2. tying a pupil to a desk

3. hanging logs around a pupil's neck

4. putting a naughty pupil in a basket hanging from the roof

5. wearing a dunce's hat

What equipment did they use?

Younger children learned to write on slates, using slate pencils. Paper was expensive but slate could be used again and again. The pupils just rubbed out the letters when they'd finished. Older pupils used paper 'copybooks' and wrote in them with a metal-nibbed wooden pen. They dipped their nibs into ink-pots and scratched the letter onto the page. They had to be careful not to spill any ink!

FACT: ▶ What about the rich kids?

▶ Rich boys were taught at home by private **tutors** until they were seven or eight years old. Then they went away to boarding school to learn Latin, Greek, Literature, History, Geography, Science and Sport. Rich girls stayed at home. They learned to sew, look after a home, cook, sing and play musical instruments.

PAUSE **FOR** **THOUGHT**

Have you ever heard of the phrase, 'You've blotted your copybook'? Where do you think it comes from?

WISE UP WORDS

dame school   ragged school   logbook   tutor

WORK

1   a   What was i) a dame school and ii) a ragged school?
    b   According to the Government, why were these schools not good enough to educate Britain's children?

2   Look at **Source A**.
    a   What were the 'three Rs'?
    b   Do you think this is a sensible name for these three subjects? Explain your answer.
    c   Why do you think boys and girls were taught different things in the afternoon?

3   Look at **Source B**.
    a   Make a list of some of the major differences between the classroom in **Source B** and the one you are sitting in.
    b   What is the biggest difference?

4   Look at **Source D**.
    a   What is a logbook?
    b   Why is Mr Brown in trouble?
    c   Why is Mrs Ferguson asked to come into school?
    d   Does anything surprise you about the last entry in the logbook?

5   Look at **Source E**.
    a   Why do you think schools had punishments like these?
    b   Which of these punishments do you think is most cruel? Give reasons for your answer.
    c   Why do you think the Government eventually banned these punishments in British schools?
    d   Should any of these punishments be re-introduced? Give reasons for your answer.

6   Imagine you are a pupil at the sort of Victorian school described in these four pages. You have been asked to prepare an *'induction leaflet'* that will be given to all new pupils starting at the school. Write your leaflet, remembering to include:
    •   Information about the sort of lessons they'll be doing.
    •   Methods of teaching and learning.
    •   A description of a typical schoolroom.
    •   Some of the rules in place and what to expect if rules are broken.
    •   A guide to the equipment in use.

Who protected Britain's citizens?

AIMS
- ▶ What is a **philanthropist**?
- ▶ How did some of Britain's best-known charities begin?
- ▶ What did the Government do to help the poorest of the poor?

In today's Britain, we think that cruelty is wrong. We all like to think that we live in a caring society where people are protected from harm. In fact, part of any Government's job is to make sure that its citizens are protected by laws.

In Victorian Britain, some people believed that the Government didn't do enough to help vulnerable people. Instead, they tried to help people themselves … and did a fantastic job. In fact, many of the charities in place today have their roots in the Victorian era.

Study **Source A** carefully. It's a poster from a recent **NSPCC** campaign called 'Protecting Babies'. The poster was designed to highlight how easily babies can be injured if they aren't handled properly. A similar TV advertisement showed an exhausted parent pushed to breaking point by a crying baby.

The campaign was a huge success – in research afterwards, eight out of ten people said that it had made them much more aware of how easily babies can be injured if not treated properly.

▼ **Source A** 'Protecting Babies' poster, part of the NSPCC's 'Cruelty to Children must stop. FULL STOP.' campaign.

A baby's arm isn't much stronger.

The NSPCC (National Society for the Prevention of Cruelty to Children) is not a new organisation – they have been actively campaigning to protect children and prevent cruelty for well over 100 years. The NSPCC, founded in 1884, is one of many examples of the fight to protect or help British citizens in Victorian times.

The terrible poverty and human suffering of the very poor haunted some people in Victorian Britain. Many decided to devote their lives to helping those less fortunate than themselves. Individuals, known as philanthropists, spent all their time helping poor people – setting up soup kitchens, care homes, hostels and schools. They worked hard to raise money and publicise the problems. Often, their work was inspired by their religious beliefs.

Look at **Source A**. i) What is the message of this poster? ii) Was this poster a success or not? Explain your answer.

FACT: ▶ Benjamin Waugh

- ▶ Founded the NSPCC in 1884 after working for the Church in the poorest parts of London. Was appalled with the treatment of children at a time when child abuse was not a criminal offence. Parents could do what they wanted with their children – the police would only get involved if the abuse ended in death!
- ▶ The NSPCC was set up to draw attention to the abuse of children. Soon, Queen Victoria was openly supporting it.

▸ Waugh worked hard, writing to the Government, raising money and writing detailed reports of abused and neglected children – until Parliament introduced some child protection laws (see **Source D**). By 1904, there were nearly 200 NSPCC inspectors with the power to remove children from abusive homes. By 1905, they had helped over one million children – and their work continues today!

FACT: ▸ Lord Shaftesbury

▸ An MP, more interested in doing good than gaining power.

▸ He was successful in leading the fight in Parliament to improve working conditions for women and children.

▸ He also campaigned to improve education and the treatment of the mentally ill (at a time when they were seen as 'circus freaks').

▸ When he died in 1885, the public collected money for a **memorial** in London. Today, it stands in the middle of Piccadilly Circus!

▾ **Source B** A chimney sweep and his six-year-old helper, photographed in the 1860s. The sweeps sent their 'climbing boys' up the narrow, twisting chimneys to sweep out the soot. Sometimes the chimneys measured just 23cm by 23cm (mark it out – it's very narrow). The boys were beaten if they took too long and sometimes got trapped and died. The soot caused cancer too. Shaftesbury is best remembered for improving conditions for young 'climbing boys' like the one in the photograph.

FACT: ▸ William Booth

▸ A preacher from a poor Nottingham family who set up the **Salvation Army** in 1865 after being horrified by the poverty in London's East End.

▸ The 'army' of volunteers, in bright uniforms, playing musical instruments, toured the poor areas of towns and cities providing clothes, food and shelter to the needy. Their 'war' (they're an army remember) was on poverty.

▸ The direct approach of the 'Sally Army' appealed to working people and support for it grew and grew. It still remains today and provides help for those in need all over the world.

▾ **Source C** Written by William Booth, 1890

'While women creep as they do now –
I'll fight,
while little children go hungry as they
do now – I'll fight,
while men go to prison, in and out, in
and out – I'll fight,
while there is a poor lost girl upon the
street – I'll fight,
while there remains a poor lost soul in
front of the light of God – I'll fight,
I'll fight – I'll fight to the very end.'

▾ **Source D** Early child protection laws

1889 Police have power to arrest abusers and enter homes of suspected abusers.

1894 Children able to give evidence in court. Mental cruelty recognised. It became an offence to deny treatment for a sick child.

1904 NSPCC inspectors given new powers to remove children from abusive homes.

Pg 108

FACT: ▶ Thomas Barnardo

▶ Thomas Barnardo set up a school for the poor in London in 1867. He opened his first home for poor children in 1870.

▶ One evening, an 11-year-old boy named John Somers (nicknamed 'Carrots') was turned away because the home was full. He was found two days later, dead from the cold! From then on, Barnardo promised never to turn away another child from his home. He had to open more and more to cope with the vast number of **destitute** children.

▶ By the time of his death in 1905, Barnardo's homes had rescued over 50 000 homeless, orphaned and crippled boys and girls. Today, **Barnardo's** is Britain's largest children's charity.

▼ **Source E** Thomas Barnardo provided boys like these with food and shelter. Amazingly, Barnardo was declared dead by two doctors when he was a baby. Only when an undertaker was about to place him in a coffin was it noticed that he was still breathing!

Today, we owe a great deal to the philanthropy of these people and they were not alone; others, like William Wilberforce and Elizabeth Fry, worked just as hard to end slavery and improve prison conditions. They drew attention to those living the most miserable lives of all and made the Government aware that it was their job to protect and help them.

FACT: ▶ The workhouse

The Government did try to help the poorest of the poor – but their help didn't always make life any better for them. In 1834, a law was passed that said that those who were old, sick or crippled could be helped at home (if they had one). But those who were fit enough to work, but didn't have a job, had to go into a **workhouse**. This was a grim, large building in each town where the poor were kept like prisoners. They were forced to work, families were separated, uniforms were worn and rules were harsh. In Andover Workhouse, workers were given the job of crushing old animal bones. In 1845, it was discovered that they were eating any flesh left on the bones because they were so hungry. To many it seemed that the poor were being punished ... for being poor!

▲ **Source F** A painting of poor people waiting to go in the workhouse.

Today, we like to think we live in a caring society. We don't tolerate abuse, cruelty, bullying or appalling living and working conditions. We are all proud of the money we raise for charity on sponsored walks, sponsored swims or Children in Need days. In many ways, we are carrying on the work of the philanthropists of Victorian Britain.

! WISE UP WORDS

NSPCC   Salvation Army   Barnardo's
philanthropists   workhouse   destitute
memorial

HUNGRY FOR MORE?

Some Victorians didn't just work hard to protect children – they tried to protect animals too.

Find out about the campaign to prevent cruelty to animals. Amazingly, there were laws to protect animals more than 50 years before there were any laws to protect children.

WORK

1 a What is a philanthropist?
   b Write no more than two sentences about each of the following:
      i) Benjamin Waugh ii) Lord Shaftesbury
      iii) William Booth iv) Thomas Barnardo
   One sentence must outline their achievements, whilst the other must mention an interesting fact.

   TOP TIP: Plan your sentences in rough first.

2 Look at **Source C**.
   In your own words, explain what Booth meant.

3 Look at **Source E**.
   a How can you tell these boys are poor?
   b Why do you think two of them are smiling? Think carefully before answering.

4 Look at **Source F**.
   a What was a workhouse?
   b Write down at least five words to describe how you think the people in the queue might be feeling. For each word, explain why you have chosen it.
   c Do you think the artist was in favour of or against workhouses? Explain your answer carefully.

Who is the man on the £10 note?

▶ Who was Charles Darwin?
▶ Why were his theories so controversial?

During the year 2000, the Bank of England chose to put Charles Darwin's face on their £10 note. They only print four bank notes (£5, £10, £20 and £50), so why was his image chosen to go on one of them? Who was this man? What did he do? And why are his achievements still remembered today?

▼ **Source A** The Bank of England £10 Darwin note. Who else appears on Bank of England notes? Make a list and then find out what each has achieved.

Charles Darwin was born in 1809, the son of a doctor from Shrewsbury. At this time, people thought the Bible was literally true. That is, that humans were God's special creation and that the world had been created in six days. In fact, a professor at Cambridge University claimed to have pinpointed the time when God created the world – 9:00am on Monday, 23 October 4004 BC! He then filled the Garden of Eden with all kinds of animals and these had stayed the same from that time on.

When Darwin was a boy, few would have disagreed with this theory. Indeed, people had believed this for centuries. Yet the number of people attending church each year was dropping. Some argued that many, especially those in towns, worked so hard that they didn't have time to go to church. Others claimed that poorer people failed to go as often because the rich were treated better in churches (see **Source B**).

▼ **Source B** A description of a church in Ipswich, 1850

'Pews for the rich were padded, lined and cushioned. The poor were seated in stools in the aisles ... and the cold damp stone beneath their feet was the only place to kneel and pray.'

In 1851, the Government did a survey of religion in England. Church leaders were shocked to discover that only 7¼ million people had gone to church recently. Although this was about 40% of the population – which seems like a lot today – Church leaders were very disappointed. They felt that more people should attend regularly.

However, church attendance continued to drop and today, Victorians would be shocked at the percentage of the population who regularly attend church on Sundays – the figure is 1%.

So how does Charles Darwin fit into all this?

In 1859, Darwin published a book, The Origin of Species, which horrified the Christian Church. In it, he suggests that life had not been created by God, as many Christians believed. Instead, he wrote that life had evolved over millions of years. His **theory of evolution** suggested that species **evolve** over many, many years, because only those best suited to their environments will survive and reproduce. Their offspring will inherit the features that helped their parents to survive. God, Darwin believed, did not have a direct influence over this!

◄ Leaves are giraffes' favourite food! The centre giraffe is taller than the giraffe on the left. What happens if the only leaves available were on the tall trees? The shorter giraffe wouldn't be able to reach, so would starve and die. The giraffe in the centre would continue to eat, live and reproduce. The new generation of giraffes would then inherit the 'tallness' gene!

Later in 1872, Darwin published The Descent of Man, in which he suggests that man evolved gradually from apes over many thousands of years. Darwin was suggesting that there did not need to be a God to explain human existence! As you can imagine, the Church attacked his ideas and newspapers were full of stories and letters mocking him. Some said his ideas were born of the devil.

◄ **Source C** Darwin and his 'friend'. This drawing **mocks** Darwin's ideas. His theories were based on years of research and a five-month voyage to the Galapagos Islands in the Pacific Ocean. He noticed that some species of birds, cut off from each other on separate islands, had developed different beaks in order to survive. They had evolved to suit their environment.

Darwin's theories are still controversial. Many people today still strongly disagree with them, but no one can deny that his ideas were thought-provoking. When Darwin died in 1882, he was buried in Westminster Abbey, London, alongside other great thinkers and writers, such as Isaac Newton and Charles Dickens. Over 100 years later, he again attracted attention from the people of Britain – as the man on the £10 note.

▼ **Source D** Based on the writings of Charles Darwin

'Bit by bit, I stopped believing in Christianity … I had always been told that animals were so wonderful that they must have been made by God. But now I know that animals have evolved over millions of years … I don't think we can ever know whether or not there is a god.'

▼ **Source E** A university professor, 1872

'Are we nothing but animals? Is that what he's saying? Is religion not true? Is being good a waste of time?'

 WISE UP WORDS

evolve   mocking   theory of evolution

WORK

1 a How many people regularly went to church in 1851?
  b Why had church attendance declined so much? Explain carefully, making sure you use a quote from **Source B** in your answer.

2 Produce your own diagram or poster that explains Darwin's theory of evolution. Use pictures where appropriate and try not to use any more than 100 words.

  TOP TIP: Aim your diagram or poster at someone of your own age who has never heard of this theory before.

3 Look at **Source C**.
  a What point is being made by this cartoon?
  b What does this cartoon tell us about people's reactions to Darwin's theories?

4 Look at **Source E**. Does the professor agree or disagree with Darwin's theory of evolution? Explain how you made your decision.

5 a Why do you think Darwin was chosen to go on the £10 note?
  b If you were asked to choose a person to go on a new note, who would it be? Make sure you give sensible reasons for your choice (and it can't be you!).

What shall I do with my leisure time?

AIMS

▶ Why did some workers get more spare time?

▶ How did people spend their time away from work?

Where did you spend your holidays this year? Did you stay at home? Go to a relative's house? Go to the seaside? Or were you lucky enough to go to a warm sunny place on the other side of the world?

The idea of families being able to 'go on holiday' is quite a new one. In 1800, few people had holidays. Sunday was their only day off so most people rested after they had been to church. Workers were given a day off for religious festivals (Christmas Day, Easter Sunday and so on) but these 'holy days' only amounted to a couple of odd days each year.

By 1850, things had started to change. People worked shorter hours than ever before and found themselves at home earlier in the evenings and off work on Saturday afternoons. All of a sudden, ordinary workers had enough **leisure time** to enjoy new sports and other pastimes, or even go away for short holidays to the seaside.

In 1871, Parliament introduced **bank holidays**, giving workers a few more days off throughout the year when banks and offices closed. Many people found themselves asking the question that they had never asked before: what am I going to do with my leisure time?

NEW SPORTS

Sports became more organised as standard rules were introduced across the country. Competitions soon followed: the FA Cup began in 1871, Wimbledon Tennis Tournament was first played in 1877 and English and Australian teams played the first Cricket Test Match in England in 1880.

◀ **Source A** The cricketer W G Grace (1848–1915), perhaps one of the most famous cricketers of all time.

NEW CRAZES

Cycling became very popular in the 1870s (it was one of the cheapest ways to travel). Even roller-skating became popular in the 1880s. Reading books became more common as more people learned how to read. New **novels** by authors such as Charles Dickens (*Oliver Twist*) and Mary Shelley (*Frankenstein*) sold thousands of copies. By the 1880s, photographs were also appearing in people's homes. It was very fashionable to go to a public park and have a family portrait taken by a street photographer.

THE SEASIDE

The railways took ordinary working-class people to the seaside to have fun. Day trips to coastal towns like Blackpool, Brighton, Southend and Margate were enjoyed by thousands of people. One of the first to realise that there was money to be made by organising rail trips was a man called Thomas Cook in the 1840s. The company still organises holidays today!

▲ **Source B** Ramsgate beach in July 1887. Can you see:
i) the pier?
ii) the Punch and Judy show?
iii) the ice cream seller?
iv) the seafront hotels?

FACT: ▶ What about blood sports?

▶ The RSPCA was set up in 1824 and the old, crueller sports slowly disappeared. Bear-baiting had been banned by 1839 and cockfighting became illegal in 1849. Public hangings were still popular but even they stopped in 1868. The last public hanging in Britain was in 1909.

HUNGRY FOR MORE?

Find out about some of the early organised sports competitions. For example:
• *Wimbledon Tennis Tournament*
• *'The Ashes' Cricket Contest*
• *The Open Golf Tournament*
• *The Calcutta Rugby Cup*

 WISE UP WORDS

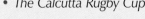
leisure time   bank holidays   novels

WORK

1 a What is 'leisure time'?
   b Why did the amount of leisure time enjoyed by many people start to increase after 1850?

2 Look at **Source B**.
   a Write a short description of this scene.
   b In what ways is the beach at Ramsgate in 1887 different from a typical British seaside beach today?

3 a What were 'blood sports'?
   b Why do you think these 'sports' gradually began to disappear?

4 It is 1890. Plan a weekend's entertainment for you and your friend and write them a letter explaining how you will both spend your time:
   • Will you watch any sports? If so, which ones?
   • What about a day at the seaside? How will you get there? Which resort? What will you do … and wear?
   • After visiting church, how will you spend Sunday afternoon? A walk in the park perhaps? What can you expect to do (and see) there?

TOP TIP: You want to make your friend excited about their visit, so your letter should be enthusiastically written!

The High Street

AIMS

▸ What did a Victorian high street look like?

▸ What are the origins of some of our now familiar high street shops?

By 1900, about 80% of the population lived in towns or cities … and they all needed a place to shop! It wasn't long before 'high street shopping' became common.

This painting, by Louise Rayner, is called The Cross, Eastgate Street, Chester. It is a great example of what a Victorian city high street would look like. Look out for:

i) The tramlines – horse-drawn tramcars ran on fixed rails along the cobblestone streets. By 1890, electric trams replaced the horse-drawn ones.

ii) Street lights – in high streets by 1835.

iii) Pavements – from the 1850s, many high street pavements were improved. The first street cleaners were employed by 1860.

iv) Street traders – as well as the shops, people could buy from street traders or **costermongers** as they were known. Can you see the costermongers in the painting? There are at least two.

v) Shops – how many different types of shop can you see?

vi) Rich men, poor men – the high street was a mixture of all types of people. Can you see the upper class men having a chat? What about the poor boys (one looking bored; the other staring through a shop window)?

High street quality

In 1875, the Food and Drugs Act made it possible for local councils to check on the quality of food on sale. The first inspectors found some amazing tricks of the trade being used by shop owners to fool their customers (like mixing river water with milk and putting sawdust into flour). Gradually, food quality improved.

New high street shops

The 1800s was the time for the birth of many of our familiar high street shops. John Sainsbury (1864), Jesse Boot (1871), William Henry Smith (1848), Michael Marks and Tom Spencer (1894) all started trading at this time. Thomas Lipton, a grocer, once said, 'Secret of my success? There isn't one, just advertise, advertise all you can. Never miss a chance of advertising.'

WISE UP WORDS

costermonger   refrigeration

Source A An early Sainsbury's store. By 1880, the invention of **refrigeration** meant that meat could be shipped from Australia and New Zealand without going mouldy. 'Fridges' inside shops meant that meat, milk and fish could be stored easily.

Source B An early Co-op shop in London

New ideas on the high street

In 1844, 28 workers from Rochdale, Lancashire, each saved up to buy a stock of food and open a shop of their own. Workers sold their goods at fair prices and shared the profits out amongst their customers. Their co-operation with each other gave its name to their first shop – 'The Co-operative'. Today, Co-ops exist all around the country.

WORK

1 a List some of the well-known shops that appeared in Victorian high streets between 1848 and 1894.

b According to Thomas Lipton, what was the secret of his success?

c Do you think this 'secret' still applies to most large stores today? Explain your answer.

2 a How did 'The Co-operative' chain of stores get its name?

b How did the 1875 Food and Drugs Act make things safer for customers?

c How did the invention of refrigeration help i) shop owners and ii) customers?

3 Prepare a guidebook for the gallery in which Louise Rayner's painting hangs. You are to write the notes that would go in the guidebook.

• Start with a basic description.

• Explain what the painting tells the viewer about life in Victorian Britain – use details from the scene to help you.

• Write why it is important to look after and preserve paintings like this.

Case study: the 1883 FA Cup Final ... and after

> ▶ Why was the 1883 FA Cup Final a turning point in English football?
> ▶ How have the rules and regulations of football changed?

Football is not a modern game: it has been popular for centuries. In the Middle Ages, whole villages played each other – and spent most of a day punching, kicking and scratching each other. For years, there weren't any proper rules, as teams just agreed them before they started. Sometimes players were allowed to handle the ball and at other times they were not. Some teams were restricted to 20 players per side, while others had up to hundreds of people per team!

Football mob!

The first official club – Sheffield – was formed in 1857. Bizarrely, there were no other official teams for them to play, so the married players played against the unmarried ones. The first professional club (a club with paid players) was Notts County, formed in 1862. Other clubs soon started and in 1863, the Football Association was set up in an attempt to get a clear set of rules written out. Once these rules were agreed (which were quite different from today's modern rules), teams sprang up all over the country. Vicars started teams because they were keen to keep local lads out of trouble (Everton, Southampton and Aston Villa started this way), and others were formed as factory sides (like Manchester United and Arsenal).

The FA Cup began in 1871 as a knockout competition open to any team in England and Wales. Teams with names like the Old Forresters, the Darwin Ramblers, the Druids and Phoenix Bessimer tried to win the trophy. So too did teams with more familiar names like Sheffield Wednesday, Nottingham Forest and Notts County. But from 1871 onwards, the first 12 FA Cup winning teams all had something in common: they were all made up of rich boys from the upper class. Try as they might, working-class teams couldn't manage to beat them.

However, the 1883 FA Cup Final was different. A team of working-class players from Blackburn had managed to reach the final ... and they were taking the match very seriously. They were due to play the cup holders, the Old Etonians, an upper-class team of former pupils from Eton, a private, fee-paying school in Surrey. This was a chance for the working-class lads to change footballing history forever.

1883 FA Cup Final

Old Etonians
(Cup holders)

v

Blackburn Olympic
(Challengers)

To be played on 31 March
at the Kensington Oval, London

Kick off: 3:00pm

Referee: Mr Crump

About 8 000 people attended the game. Newspaper reporters from Blackburn and Eton were in the crowd, there to write stories for their local papers. Read the following newspaper report carefully. Can you work out whether it would have appeared in a Blackburn paper or an Eton one?

Source A The Chronicle newspaper, 1883

The Chronicle

1 April 1883

Bruising Blackburn beat brave Etonians

KICKING THE DECISIVE GOAL.

Crossley scores the decisive goal

There are new FA Cup champions today. The Old Etonians have lost their crown to a bruising Blackburn Olympic side. After winning last year's tournament, beating Blackburn Rovers, the Old Etonians were favourites to retain their trophy. However, they didn't expect the fouling tactics of the working-class boys from the small factory town of Blackburn, Lancashire.

In the first half, the play of the Old Etonians was too casual and they should have scored several goals while fresh. Despite this, as half-time approached, they managed to take the lead with a goal by Harry Goodhart. It was a superb goal too. During half-time, the Blackburn players were shouted at so much by their manager that some Eton players listening outside their opponents' dressing room were embarrassed by the foul and abusive language. When they returned to the pitch, the Blackburn players looked angry and improved their play.

Shortly after half-time, Arthur Dunn, the Old Etonian and England International, was forced to leave the field after being thrown to the ground. Then a knocking out spirit seemed to affect Blackburn Olympic as they fouled the Old Etonian team repeatedly.

The Blackburn men equalled the score mid-way through the second half, with a fortunate goal from Andrew Matthews. The rough play continued but the full-time score was 1–1.

When extra time began, the Etonian forwards were tired and a winning goal, scored by Jimmy Crossley, gave Blackburn Olympic victory. It was a poor shot which only just crept over the line before Rawlinson in the Eton goal could react.

Major Marindin, President of the FA, presented the cup and called for three cheers. The cheers were not loud at the ground, but the cheers in Blackburn must have been deafening. Old Etonians will probably gain revenge next year.

▶ **Source B** The winning captain, Sam Warburton

PAUSE FOR THOUGHT

Did you work it out? You will probably have noticed that the newspaper report is very biased – it favours one side more than the other. What words or phrases made you think that the report was written by an Eton reporter rather than a Blackburn one?

119

The 1883 FA Cup Final was a turning point in English football history. For the first time, a truly working-class football team had won the cup. Never again would a team of upper-class players reach the FA Cup Final.

FACT: ▶ Cups and coins

▸ The FA Cup was won by working-class teams from the North or Midlands for the next 12 years. In 1895, the cup was stolen from a shop window in Birmingham after it was won by Aston Villa. The cup was never found and a new one was made. In 1958, a former criminal admitted stealing the cup in 1895 and melting it down to make fake coins.

In 1888, the first football league was set up by 12 'founding' clubs. Soon other clubs wanted to join so the FA decided to introduce more leagues.

▾ **Source C** The final placings for the first ever football league

	P	W	D	L	F	A	Pts
Preston North End	22	18	4	0	74	15	40
Aston Villa	22	12	5	5	61	43	29
Wolverhampton Wanderers	22	12	4	6	50	37	28
Blackburn Rovers	22	10	6	6	66	45	26
Bolton Wanderers	22	10	2	10	63	59	22
West Bromwich Albion	22	10	2	10	40	46	22
Accrington	22	6	8	8	48	48	20
Everton	22	9	2	11	35	46	20
Burnley	22	7	3	12	42	62	17
Derby County	22	7	2	13	41	60	16
Notts County	22	5	2	15	39	73	12
Stoke	22	4	4	14	26	51	12

Huge crowds were drawn to these early games, mainly due to the fact that mines and factories now closed at midday on Saturdays. For the first time, workers had the free time to attend Saturday afternoon games. The railways also helped the popularity of the sport because it was easier than ever before for a 'fan' to travel around the country following their team. Also, young people were attracted to the sport because it was cheap to play – little equipment was needed and it could be played at any time in almost any weather. It soon became known as 'the people's game'.

The growing popularity of football was confirmed in 1901 when a crowd of 110 000 people watched the FA Cup Final at Selhurst Park, London.

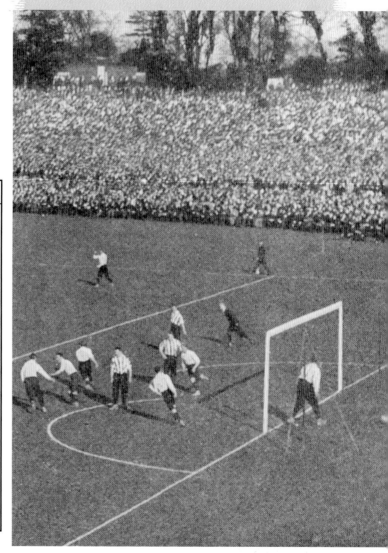

▾ **Source D** The 1901 FA Cup Final: Tottenham Hotspur score against Sheffield United.

Football's rules and regulations continued to change until the game began to resemble the one we are familiar with today. Indeed, Association Football (as it is correctly known or 'soccer' as it's nicknamed) remains England's national sport and is now one of the best known and most loved sports in the world.

▼ **Source E** Arthur Wharton (1865–1930) was the world's first professional black footballer. He played professional cricket too! Born in Cannock, Staffordshire, he also held the world record for the 100-yard sprint between 1886 and 1887.

▼ **Source F** Key developments and events in the history of football

Date	Event
1866	Ball size fixed
1870	Only 11 players allowed per team
1872	Referee first used (but only to keep time)
1872	First international between England and Scotland
1873	Free kick awarded for handball
1874	First use of shin pads
1874	Referees given power to send off players
1875	Crossbar used instead of tape
1878	Referees used whistle for the first time
1878	First floodlit match
1882	Two-handed throw in introduced
1885	Highest ever score recorded in a British game. Arbroath beat Bon Accord in the Scottish Cup 36–0
1889	Ball weight fixed
1891	Goal nets used for the first time
1891	Penalty kick introduced

WORK

1 a Draw this puzzle in your book and fill in the answers to the clues.

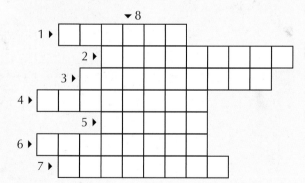

Clues:

1 _____ Ramblers – early football team
2 World's first official club
3 _____ Olympic – first working class winners of FA Cup
4 Football's traditional day
5 Bottom team in 1888
6 36–0 winners
7 Leg protectors, first used in 1874

 b Now read *down* the puzzle (clue 8). Write a sentence or two about this person.

2 Look at **Sources D** and **E** and the news article on page 119. Make a list of the similarities and differences between a modern game of football and the images shown in these sources.

TOP TIP: Think about kit, crowds, stadia, pitches and so on.

3 a How did i) the Government and ii) the railways help the popularity of football?
 b You might need an atlas for this task. On a basic map of Britain, mark where all the teams in the first ever Football League were based.
 c What do you notice about the areas where these teams are based?

4 a You may have noticed that the news report on page 119 is very biased. It was clearly written by a reporter who supported the Old Etonians and wasn't too keen on Blackburn Olympic. Now write a news report from the point of view of a Blackburn Olympic supporter. Imagine you are writing for the *Blackburn Post* and have been an Olympic fan for years.
 b Give examples of how your report is different from the report on page 119.

How did Britain change from 1750 to 1900?

 AIM ▶What important ideas and inventions appeared between 1750 and 1900?

This book covers the years 1750 to 1900. During this time, some amazing and lasting changes took place. It was a period in British history when great industrial towns and cities appeared, full of people linked together by roads, canals and trains that ran through the countryside. By 1900, most people were better fed, clothed, healthier and more educated than anyone could have imagined in 1750. Shops contained goods from all over the world, brought to Britain in huge steamships, which stood in newly built docks.

Today's Britain is full of reminders from this period. If you look around any town or city, you will see bridges, railways, stations, pubs, statues, libraries, churches, town halls and even school buildings that were designed and built between 1750 and 1900. Some of you may even live in houses built during this time. Much of what we take for granted today – light bulbs, cameras, motor cars, telephones, post boxes, even the basic rules of sports like rugby, cricket and football – came from the period covered in this book.

Read this section carefully. It doesn't feature all the changes, discoveries and inventions that took place between 1750 and 1900, but it tries to pick out some of the most important and interesting ones.

1750	1900
Travel: Very slow. London to Edinburgh = two weeks by road.	**Travel**: Much faster. London to Edinburgh = nine hours by train.

1750	1900
Leisure time: Working people had few holidays. Blood sports very popular.	**Leisure time**: Working people enjoyed shorter working hours and therefore more leisure time. Sports became more organised.

1750
Population: 7 million
80% lived in the countryside.

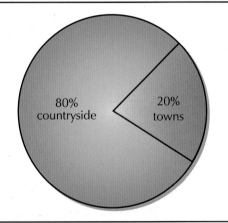

80% countryside   20% towns

1900
Population: 37 million
80% lived in towns and cities.

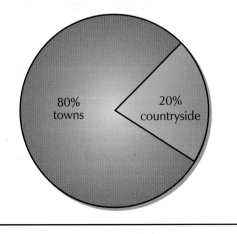

80% towns   20% countryside

1750	1900
Health and medicine: People didn't know that germs caused disease. If a person reached the age of one, they might expect to live to the age of 40.	**Health and medicine:** Discovered that germs caused disease. Inventions such as vaccinations, antiseptic and anaesthetics meant that if you reached the age of one, you might expect to live to the age of 55.

1750	1900
Politics: Only 5% of the population could vote in elections. No women could vote.	**Politics:** Now most men could vote, but still no women could vote.

1750	1900
The British Empire	**The British Empire**

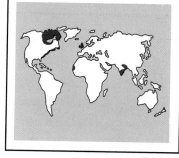

▼ **Source A** Coca-Cola was one of the many now familiar products and inventions that appeared between 1750 and 1900. Others include Christmas cards (1842), Levi jeans (1874), the telephone (1876), motor cars (1885, invented by a German, Karl Benz), bras (1889), zips (1891) and breakfast cereals (1895 – Shredded Wheat).

Coca-Cola (1885) was invented by a chemist who was looking for a headache cure. It was named after its original ingredients – coca leaves (also used to make cocaine!) and kola nuts.

WORK

1 a Copy one of the sentences below that best describes Britain in 1900:
 - Britain had changed completely between 1750 and 1900.
 - Britain had changed a lot by 1900, but some things had not changed.
 - Britain had not changed at all between 1750 and 1900.

 b Explain your choice of sentence. Use the information on these two pages and anything else you have learned whilst studying this period to help support your answer.

2 One of the world's most famous newspapers, *The Times*, first appeared on sale in 1785. In small groups, produce your own *Times*, but write it to cover the whole period 1750 to 1900. Write articles for each of the following headlines:
 - Living and working
 - The fight for rights
 - Crime and punishment
 - Sports pages
 - Designers, inventors and engineers
 - Health news
 - Women's page
 - The Empire
 - Getting around

3 Why not find out more about some of the products and inventions mentioned on this double page? Prepare factfiles on some (or all) of them.

Have you been learning?

Task 1

Here are ten sentences. Each sentence has two errors. One is a spelling mistake; the other is a factual error. When you have spotted the mistakes, write the sentence out correctly.

a The Ludites were a group of protesters who went around setting fire to farm buildings.

b The People's Charter was a list of 12 demands which called for changes to the voting sistem.

c John Snow, a miner from Londan, worked out the cause of cholera in 1854.

d In 1858, Joseph Bazalgette began work on a system of sewers that were to run under Manchester and carry away 420 million gallons of sewage a day. Many of the sewars are still in use today!

e The discovery of anaesthetics and anteseptics made operations much cleaner and safer. Anaesthetics killed germs whilst antiseptics put patients to sleep for a short while.

f The NSPCC started in 1884. It was set up to protect animals and prevent crualty.

g The world's most famous football compitition, the FA Cup, began in 1877.

h The Wimbledon Cricket Tournamnet was first played in 1877.

i Blackpool, Brighton, Southend, Margate and Birmingham all became popular seaside resorts in Victorian times.

j Wolverhampton Wanderers won the first ever Football League in 1888. The league contained 12 teems.

Task 2

a Here are six groups of words and names. In each group there is an odd one out. When you think you have found it, write a sentence or two to explain why you think it doesn't fit in with any of the others.

i) secret voting • all men over 21 to vote • all women over 21 to vote • an election every year

ii) vaccination • anaesthetic • antiseptic • antibiotics

iii) dame school • comprehensive school • ragged school • private school

iv) RSPCA • Salvation Army • NSPCC • Dr Barnardo's

v) Boots • WHSmith • Marks & Spencer • Body Shop

vi) Blackburn Rovers • Aston Villa • Liverpool • Everton

b Now make up your own 'odd one out' word sets. Make three sets and then try them out on a classmate – can they find the odd one out?

Task 3

a Complete the following names and places from your studies of 1750–1900. Look at the clues and write out the words, making sure you fill in the missing consonants.

i) _ d w _ r d J _ n n _ r
(smallpox vaccination)

ii) D _ ck T _ rp _ n
(highwayman)

iii) J _ hn Mc _ d _ m
(road builder)

iv) t _ rn p _ k _ r _ _ d
(pay a toll to use it)

v) J _ s _ _ h W _ dgw _ _ d
(pottery maker)

vi) Th _ Br _ dg _ w _ t _ r C _ n _ l
(Britain's first long, narrow, man-made channel of water)

vii) L _ v _ rp _ _ l t _ M _ nch _ st _ r R _ _ lw _ y
(first intercity railroad)

viii) Th _ Gr _ _ t _ xh _ b _ t _ _ n
(Albert's idea)

ix) tr _ nsp _ rt _ t _ _ n
(sent overseas)

x) _ l _ z _ b _ th Fry
(prison reformer)

xi) 'J _ ck th _ R _ pp _ r'
(never caught)

xii) C _ th _ r _ n _ _ dd _ ws
(one of his victims)

Task 4

a Draw this puzzle in your book and fill in the answers to the clues:

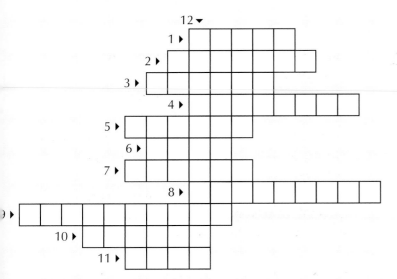

1 'The Great _____' – smelly London in 1858
2 Killer disease
3 Means 'dirty air'
4 Crapper – made fine _____ toilets
5 World record holder … for amputation
6 Robert _____ – kind factory owner
7 Greek word for 'rotten'
8 Still Britain's largest children's society
9 Means 'passed on by touch'
10 John Snow's profession
11 Salvation _____ – Booth's idea

b Now read *down* the puzzle (clue 12). Write a sentence or two about this famous man.

Task 5

Note making is an important skill. To do it successfully, you must pick out any key words in each sentence. The key words are the ones that are vital to the meaning of the sentence. Without these words, the sentence makes no sense.

For example: 'Arthur Wharton, who lived from 1865 to 1930, world's first professional black footballer. He played professional cricket too!'

The key words are: Arthur Wharton; 1865 to 1930; world's first professional black footballer; cricket.

a Now write down the key words in the following sentences. The key words are your notes.

- Between 1750 and 1840, there were over 700 full-scale riots in Britain.
- Some of the riots were started by men who were unhappy that only a small number of rich men were allowed to vote in elections.
- As the riots got more and more violent, Parliament allowed a few more to vote. However, by 1832, Parliament allowed only one in five men to vote … and no women.
- One of the most famous groups to demand the right to vote was the Chartists. They collected millions of signatures on a petition that demanded changes to the voting system.
- They also organised a huge meeting in London in 1848, which worried the Government so much they sent Queen Victoria to the Isle of Wight! However, not many went to the meeting because it rained.
- Eventually, over several years, Parliament gave more and more people the vote. By 1884, every British man held the right to vote.
- However, all women didn't have the right to vote until 1928.

b Why not make notes on other topics or parts of your work notes?

Task 6

There are two parts to this task.
i) Work through the ten 'firsts' featured below, finding out the date of each one.
ii) Then put the 'firsts' in chronological order.
   a first telephone
   b first Sainsbury's store
   c the world's first railway locomotive, built by Richard Trevithick
   d Arkwright's first factory opens
   e the world's first iron bridge is built
   f first Cricket Test Match between England and Australia
   g first Wimbledon Tennis Tournament
   h world's first official police force goes into action
   i world's first football league is won
   j the world's first international exhibition

pg l

Glossary

Abolish/abolition   To bring an end/to do away with. For example, the slave trade.

Aboriginal   A person who lived in Australia and Tasmania before the British arrived.

Acts   Laws passed by Parliament.

Alcoholic   Someone who is addicted to alcohol.

Amputate   To cut off a part of the body, such as a leg or arm.

Anaesthetic   A substance that stops you feeling pain.

Antiseptic   A chemical that prevents infection by killing germs.

Aqueduct   A bridge that carries a canal over an obstacle (such as a river).

Arthritis   Painful swelling of the joints and muscles.

Auction   A public sale in which goods are sold to the person who offers the highest price.

Back-to-back   Rows of houses, built very close together with no room for a garden.

Ballot   Vote.

Bank holidays   One-day holidays, introduced by Parliament in 1871.

Barnardo's   A children's charity, aimed at helping homeless, orphaned or crippled boys and girls.

Bearers   A mining job: children who carry coal-sacks around the pit.

Black lung   A nickname for a miner's illness that resulted in coughing fits and shortness of breath.

Blight   A disease that makes plants die, usually caused by bacteria or fungi.

Branded   Permanently marked by burning skin with a hot metal instrument. The mark showed who owned the slave.

Canal   A long, narrow, man-made channel of water.

Canal mania   A time between 1761 and about 1830 when many canals were built all over Britain.

Candidate   A person who is being considered for a job. The job could be as a Member of Parliament.

Cannibals   People who eat human flesh.

Carding   Combing or untangling wool before spinning.

Cast iron   Iron that has been heated into a liquid and placed in a mould to make a shape.

Census   Official count of the population, done every ten years in Britain.

Chartists   A group who demanded changes to the voting system between 1837 and 1848. They were called Chartists after their six-point charter, or list of demands.

Chloroform   A strong smelling liquid that was used as an anaesthetic.

Cholera   A deadly disease caused by infected food or water. Victims suffer from diarrhoea, vomiting and can die.

Clerk   A person whose job is to keep records or accounts in an office, bank or court.

Clothier   A person who buys and sells cloth.

Coalface   The area where coal is dug out of the ground.

Coining   Making fake coins or shaving bits of metal away from the edges of coins in order to make other ones with the bits.

Colony   An area of land somewhere in the world ruled by Britain.

Constable   An unpaid person who tried to keep law and order in his town for a period of one year.

Constipation   Unable to go to the toilet properly.

Contagionists   People who believed that disease was passed on by touching people or things infected with it.

Contagious   Spreading by contact; catching.

Contaminated   If something is contaminated by dirt or chemicals, it is made harmful.

Costermonger   A street trader.

Dame school   A basic school run by women, often in the front room of their house. Pupils paid a few pennies to attend.

Dehydrate   To become weak through losing too much water from the body.

Democracy   A system of running a country. In a democracy, the people vote for the political party they want to make decisions on their behalf.

Domestic system   The system where people worked in their homes or small workshops rather than in factories.

Drawers   A mining job: children who push and pull loaded coal wagons in the pit.

Emigrated   Moved to another country to live.

Empire   A collection of colonies all ruled by one 'mother country'.

Enclosed farms   Farms made up of strips of land. Large 'enclosed farms' were formed when one farmer bought strips of land from other farmers.

Engineer   A person who plans and builds machines, roads, buildings and so on.

Entrepreneur   A business person who takes risks, often with their own money, in order to make a profit.

Epidemic   Rapid spread of a disease.

Ether   A colourless liquid that was used as an anaesthetic.

Evolve   Gradual change.

Exported   Sent out to other countries, usually to be sold.

Factory system   The system where people worked in factories to produce goods in large numbers that used to be produced in people's homes or in small workshops. Replaced the domestic system.

Flying shuttle   A 1733 invention in the cloth industry, which speeded up weaving.

Fuller   A person who cleans, bleaches, shrinks and presses cloth.

Gallows   A wooden frame used for hanging criminals.

Gruel   A type of porridge, eaten by prisoners.

Home Secretary   The Government official responsible for law and order.

Immigration   Coming to a foreign country in order to settle there.

Imported   Brought in from another country, usually to be sold.

Impurities   Dirty or unwanted materials mixed in with a substance.

Independence   Existing separately from other people or things. An independent nation has no help from another country.

Indifferent   Not bothered, showing no interest. Poor quality.

Industrial Revolution   A complete change in the way things were made. A time when factories replaced farming as the main form of business in Britain. Sometimes used to describe the changes in population, transport, cities and so on in the period between 1750 and 1900.

Industry   The work and methods involved in making things in factories.

Inferior   Lower than.

International   Involving different countries.

Ironworks   A factory that makes things from iron.

Laissez faire   A French word meaning 'leave alone'.

Lashed   Whipped.

Leisure time   Spare time to do the things you enjoy.

Literacy   Ability to read and write.

Locomotive   An engine used to pull trucks or passenger carriages along a track.

Logbook   An official record of the school.

Loom   A machine for weaving cloth.

Maintenance   The process of keeping something the same or in good condition.

Manufacture   To make goods in a factory.

Maori   A person who lived in New Zealand before the British arrived.

Maternity   Relating to or involving pregnant women and birth.

Mechanised   If work is mechanised, machines are installed to do it.

Miasmatists   People who believed that disease was passed on by dirty air (miasma).

Middle class   People between the upper and working classes, such as doctors, lawyers, factory managers and so on.

Midwives   Nurses trained to help women at the birth of a baby.

Miners   Workers who dig coal out of the ground.

Missionaries   People of a certain religion who go to other countries to try to make converts.

Mocking   Teasing; making fun of.

Mortuary   A building where dead people are stored until they are buried.

Muzzle   A cover or strap that covers up the nose and mouth.

Natives   People who lived in a particular place before Europeans arrived.

Natural resource   A feature of the environment that is needed and used by people, for example, coal, gas, oil and so on.

Navvies   Workers employed to build roads, railways, canals or buildings.

Novels   Long, fictitious stories in book form.

NSPCC   National Society for the Prevention of Cruelty to Children. A charity that attempts to help vulnerable children.

Nystagmus   An eye illness caused by many years of straining to see in poor light.

Okra   A tropical plant with long green edible pods.

Overseer   A man in charge of the workers on a day-to-day basis, like a manager.

Pacify   Soothe or calm.

Pardoned   Officially released from punishment for a crime.

Patent   An official right given to an inventor to be the only person or company allowed to make, sell or use a new product.

Pauper apprentice   An orphan who works in a factory in return for food and a bed.

The People's Charter   The name given to the list of six demands that the Chartists hoped would give ordinary people political rights.

Petition   A document demanding change and signed by a lot of people.

Philanthropist   Someone who freely gives help or money to people in need.

Piracy   Being a pirate, a person who robs people at sea.

Plantation   A huge farm that grows cotton, sugar, tobacco and so on. A plantation owner usually uses slaves to do the work.

Pleads her belly   A plea by a woman on trial for a crime. If she pleads her belly, it means she is claiming to be pregnant and asking to be found not guilty of the crime.

Poaching   Catching animals illegally on someone else's land.

Population   The number of people in a particular place at a particular time.

Power loom   A 1787 invention in the cloth industry, which speeded up weaving. Used steam power.

Prime Minister   The leader of the biggest political party in Parliament – the leader of the Government.

Prostitute   A person, usually a woman, who has sex with men in exchange for money.

Ragged school   A charity school, which was free to attend for very poor children.

Rally   A huge meeting.

Raw materials   Natural substances, such as coal, iron ore, gold, oil and so on.

Rebel   To fight against the Government or other authority. A rebel fights against something and behaves differently from other people.

Recruited   Asked or found to join a group or organisation.

Reformers   People who want things (like living or working conditions) to change for the better.

Refrigeration   A way of keeping something very cold in order to preserve it.

Restraint   Calm, controlled behaviour.

Revolt   A violent attempt by a group of people to change the people who rule them.

Rheumatism   Painful stiffness in joints and muscles.

Ripperologist   A person who studies the crimes of 'Jack the Ripper'.

Rotary motion   Moving in a circular direction.

Rural   Countryside.

Ruts   Deep holes in roads.

Salvation Army   A charity organisation set up in 1865 by William Booth. Volunteers toured the poorer parts of cities and towns providing food, shelter and clothing to those in need.

Scramble   A method of buying slaves. A price is agreed before the buyers rush into a cage to grab the best slave they can.

Sepsis   Poisoning or infection.

Slave trader   A person who buys and sells slaves.

Smallpox   A disease that causes a fever and a rash. Victims can die.

Spinning frame   A 1769 invention in the cloth industry, which increased the supply of strong, thick thread. Used water, then steam power and needed to be housed in a factory.

Spinning jenny   A 1764 invention in the cloth industry, which increased the supply of thread.

Spinning mule   A 1779 invention in the cloth industry, which increased the supply of strong, fine thread. Used steam power.

Spinning wheel   A machine that spins wool or cotton into fine threads (yarn).

Squalor   Filthy living conditions.

Steam engine   An engine that uses steam as a means of power.

Sterilised   A sterilised object is free from any germs.

Suburb   An area of a town or city that is away from the centre.

Superior   Better position.

Surplus   An amount left over.

Tar   A thick, black, sticky substance that dries hard and is used to cover roads.

Terrace   A row of houses.

Theory of evolution   An idea that humans develop slowly from single-cell creatures over millions of years. It is the opposite of the 'creation' theory, which believes God made the world.

Toll   An amount of money charged for using a stretch of road or a bridge.

Toll keeper   A man who collects money (tolls) so that travellers can use a turnpike road.

Tories   One of the top two political parties in the eighteenth and nineteenth centuries. Generally less in favour of change.

Trade Union   An organisation or group of workers that try to improve the pay and conditions in their particular industry or place of work.

Transportation   A punishment. Guilty criminals could be sent to a far away land for a period of 5, 7 or 14 years.

Trappers   A mining job: children who open and close trapdoors in the pit.

Truncheon   A thick, wooden stick that policemen carry as a weapon.

Tuberculosis   A deadly infection that attacks the lungs.

Turnpike trust   A group of businessmen who improve and maintain a stretch of road and charge people to use it.

Tutor   A teacher.

Typhoid   An infectious disease caused by contaminated water or food. Victims have a fever and can die.

Typhus   An infectious disease passed on by lice. Victims have a fever, headaches and a rash.

Uncivilised   Unacceptable, for example, by being very rude or cruel.

Upper class   The richest people in the land – dukes, duchesses, lords and ladies.

Vaccination   The process of giving someone a vaccine (a substance made from the germs that cause the disease), usually by injection, which protects you against disease by making you immune to it.

Viaduct   A long, high bridge that carries a road or railway across an obstacle (such as a valley or river).

Viceroy   King or queen's representative who rules another part of the world on their behalf.

Watchman   A paid volunteer who tried to catch criminals.

Whigs   One of the top two political parties in the eighteenth and nineteenth centuries. Generally more in favour of reform.

Whore   An offensive, insulting word, used as an alternative for the word 'prostitute'.

Workhouse   A building where poor people were sent if they wanted food and clothing.

Working class   Poorer people who worked for a living – factory workers, miners, servants and so on.

Wrought iron   Iron that has been heated up and hammered into shape. More flexible than cast iron.

Yam   A vegetable that grows in hot regions. Also called a sweet potato.

Yarn   Thread used for knitting or making cloth.